THE GOD
OF THE OLD TESTAMENT
IN RELATION TO WAR

By
MARION J. BENEDICT, Ph.D.

Teachers College, Columbia University
Contributions to Education, No. 263

WIPF & STOCK · Eugene, Oregon

Wipf and Stock Publishers
199 W 8th Ave, Suite 3
Eugene, OR 97401

Edward Irving
Man, Preacher, Prophet
By Root, Jean Christie
ISBN 13: 978-1-60899-376-5
Publication date 1/21/2010
Previously published by Sherman, French & Co, 1912

To my Parents

ACKNOWLEDGMENTS

The writer desires to acknowledge her deep indebtedness to Professor George A. Coe, the chairman of her dissertation committee, for the privilege of her years of study under the constant stimulus of his keen and fearless thinking, and for his wholehearted interest and invaluable guidance in the present work. The writer wishes also to thank the other members of her committee—Professor Julius A. Bewer, Professor Willystine Goodsell, and Professor Adelaide T. Case—for the ideal of scholarship presented to her through their teaching, and for their careful and highly suggestive criticism of this study.

M. J. B.

CONTENTS

CHAPTER		PAGE
I.	INTRODUCTION	1
II.	THE EARLIEST HEBREW LITERATURE	10
	1. Early Poetic Fragments	10
	2. Early Narrative of the Establishment of the Kingdom	14
	3. The Book of the Acts of Solomon	19
	4. Early Laws	21
III.	NARRATIVES FROM THE NINTH AND EIGHTH CENTURIES	23
	1. Narratives from the Ninth Century Now Incorporated in the Books of Kings	23
	2. The J Document	27
	3. The E Document	36
IV.	PRE-EXILIC PROPHETS	44
	1. Amos	44
	2. Hosea	48
	3. Isaiah	51
	4. Micah	57
	5. The Deuteronomists	59
	6. Zephaniah	66
	7. Nahum	68
	8. Habakkuk	69
	9. Jeremiah	70
V.	WRITINGS FROM THE EXILIC PERIOD	76
	1. Ezekiel	76
	2. Holiness Code	81
	3. Lamentations	83
	4. Other Fragments of Poetry and Prophecy	87
	5. Historical Writings with the Point of View of Deuteronomy	90
	6. Deutero-Isaiah	94
VI.	WRITINGS FROM THE FIRST CENTURY AFTER THE RESTORATION	99
	1. Prophetic Work in the Early Restoration Period	99
	2. The P Document	106
	3. Further Prophetic Work	112
	4. Memoirs of Nehemiah and of Ezra	116
	5. Ruth	118

CHAPTER		PAGE
VII.	PROPHECY AND NARRATIVE FROM THE LATE PERSIAN AND EARLY GREEK PERIODS	122
	1. Joel and Other Prophetic Fragments	122
	2. Esther	126
	3. Chronicles	128
	4. Jonah	133
VIII.	WISDOM LITERATURE AND POETIC ANTHOLOGIES	136
	1. Job, Proverbs, Ecclesiastes, Song of Songs	136
	2. Psalms	144
	3. Appendix to Discussion of Psalms	152
IX.	PROPHECY FROM THE SECOND CENTURY	157
	1. Daniel	157
	2. Other Prophecies	160
X.	EDUCATIONAL IMPLICATIONS	163
	1. Old Testament Resources for Education with regard to Peace and War	163
	2. Suggestions as to Curriculum Policies	181
	BIBLIOGRAPHY	185

THE GOD OF THE OLD TESTAMENT IN RELATION TO WAR

CHAPTER I

INTRODUCTION

In Channing Pollock's play, *The Enemy*, Professor Arndt, himself a pacifist, refers to the Bible as "the worst of all pacifist books," and to the command, "Thou shalt not kill," as "the worst of all pacifist lines." When Mizzi remonstrates: "But that just means killing . . . *someone*," he replies with gentle sarcasm: "I see. You think it was written for the retail trade!"

Is it true that the Bible is "the worst of all pacifist books"? With regard to the problem of peace-making, can the Bible be treated as a "book," with the implied assumption of uniformity of attitude, or is it rather a library, composed of writings presenting widely variant viewpoints? When such a pronouncement as "Thou shalt not kill" is discovered in this literature, does it, in its context, refer to "the retail trade," or does it inescapably hold for the fair-minded reader that broader significance for society which Professor Arndt finds in it?

Such questions as these assume educational importance to-day on account of certain fundamental aspects of our thinking. The problem of attitudes toward war thrusts itself into numerous phases of national and community and individual life. There is no consensus of opinion as to the necessity for war, or as to the policies most likely to prevent war, but it is safe to say that comparatively few people to-day actually desire war.

The possibility of shaping the attitudes and conduct of a social group through a consistent educational process is generally admitted. Hence, attitudes toward war on the part of the youth of any community or nation could conceivably be strongly influenced by our organized educational agencies if they were so directed as to express consistently a definite point of view on this problem.

2 The God of the Old Testament in Relation to War

Educators are increasingly tending to select material on account of its probable contribution to meeting the actual life needs of the group which is being educated, rather than because of some supposed intrinsic value in certain material, whatever the background or present problems or future situation of the ones using it. The Bible has in the past held a prominent place in education, often with the assumption that all parts of its material have a sort of absolute educational value per se. It is still the main element in the material of religious education and often plays some part in secular education under the state, but those who so use it may in fairness be challenged to-day to demonstrate and analyze its contribution to individual and group life. (Since the Bible is a collection of writings arising from varied situations covering a long period of time—writings now regarded as exhibiting changing ethical and religious ideas—the different parts of the Biblical material might vary greatly in their usefulness in regard to any particular present-day problem of ethics or religion.

Therefore, if attitudes toward war to-day constitute an important and inescapable problem, it is essential for educators who would utilize Biblical material to evaluate the probable influence of the different parts of this material in shaping these sented as willing it or participating in it.[1]

Further, it is essential that within this larger problem the attitudes toward war implied in the conception of God be studied.

The conception of God in any writing arises out of the past and present experience of the group from whose life the writing comes, qualified by the personal experience of the individual writer. Until *something* in this experience leads to a questioning of the rightness (individual expediency, or social validity) of any attitude or any element in conduct, God will not be portrayed as condemning it. Hence, as long as war was an accepted factor in human experience, God was naturally represented as willing it or participating in it.[1]

[1] Cf. Cadbury, *National Ideals in the Old Testament*, pp. 66-68. "Like much of modern society, the ancient Hebrew looked upon war as a necessary evil. . . . The origin of war seemed no more artificial than the causes of rain and earthquake; all three were assigned to supernatural causes. . . . As the way to international peace only two paths occurred to them: a world empire based on conquest, and the intervention of God. Either the mailed fist and

Introduction

Professor Coe's conclusion as to the genesis of the god-idea will carry us a step further. He finds it "a spontaneous, underived conviction that what is most important for us is *really* important, that is, respected and provided for by the reality upon which we depend."[2] There exists the "perennial tendency of religion to anthropomorphize the world, peopling it with spirits and gods; likewise its tendency to sum up and represent social organization, social purpose, and social protest in such beings."[3] This "social protest" is the dominant aspect of the creative periods in the development of the conception of God in any religion. The ethical prophet, through the religious experience which is essentially "a revaluation of values, . . . a change in desire and in the ends of conduct," reaches a new stage in the evolution of the idea of the God who embodies his social values, and then, in the name of his God, "calls upon the people to like what they do not like."[4] Eventually other men come to accept this "social ethical thought of God that causes discomfort to those who seriously entertain it." At any creative period of a religion, then, the tendency is to think of God as the embodiment of the highest values yet conceived through the social experience of the individuals concerned. To be "like God" would be to express in conduct supremely desirable social attitudes.[5]

At these creative periods in the evolution of a religion, the protagonist of a new ideal is often impelled to commit to writing the conceptions which he is striving to make the social group accept. From writings of this nature come many of those finally considered to be "sacred." The evolutionary process continues, however; another creative personality influences the religion, and then eventually another and another. With developing ethical sensitiveness, the ideals of a group at any particular time

---

pan-Hebraism, or else such a divine miracle as should include within its scope the taming of martial men and the transformation of the lion and the adder—these two seemed the only sure curatives for war. So fully did the ancient Hebrew accept as a human necessity the will to fight. In like manner, the efficiency of war does not seem to have been questioned more in antiquity than in modern times. [As much?] . . . The absence of any recognized alternative to war was a chief reason that the institution's efficiency was unchallenged."

[2] Coe, George A., *The Psychology of Religion*, p. 106.
[3] *Ibid.*, p. 250.
[4] *Ibid.*, p. 222.
[5] Cf. McGiffert, *The God of the Early Christians*, pp. 184 f., for the use of the conception of the "imitation of God" by early Christian writers.

may have advanced beyond the ideals of a past period which gave rise to certain writings regarded as "sacred," or "inspired." In such a case, the conception of God in some "inspired" writing may fall below the ethical ideals of a group using this writing, and, if it is presented as authoritative, "religion" may hinder ethical progress. This in no way implies that earlier stages of development should not be studied, if recognized as such. As Badé well points out, "the harm lies not in dealing with imperfect moral standards, but in the failure to recognize them as imperfect." [6]

It is conceivable, then, that in the case of the Biblical literature some parts may present a conception of God below our present ideal of values in human life, while other parts may portray an ideal far beyond anything that has actually been attained by any social group. We shall need to investigate the conception of God in each writing in order to discover whether this is the case. If it proves to be, then either to use or to reject the Biblical material without discrimination on this point would be to rob the present generation of one of its most effectual sources of challenge and inspiration. Those who plan curricula of religious education cannot fulfill their function unless they have in mind an analysis of the material that will make possible such selection and treatment of its various parts as will best further the particular aims of their work, whether those aims point toward war-like or peace-making attitudes.

Two other considerations that bear on the significance of the problem of the relation of God to war may be noted at this point.

In a stage of thought which is frankly henotheistic, a certain god's care for just one nation is to be expected. When the conception of that god's control is widened to include all nations or even any others, his continued partiality for one assumes a different aspect. Special love and care for one over against the others can, it would seem, in no way be justified. When situations or statements involving attributes of a henotheistic god of the Hebrews are treated as though they referred to one God of the whole world, we create one of the most serious problems of

---

[6] Badé, *The Old Testament in the Light of To-day*, p. 5.

theodicy for the present day. The ease with which "Christian nations" at war slip into this stage of partial henotheism has been demonstrated on countless occasions. Dr. Gilbert offers an illuminating array of evidence as to the belief of both sides, in the American Civil War and in the Boer War, that God was fighting with their armies.[7] Since the writing of this book in 1914, the World War has furnished other striking illustrations.

In the second place, there is a subtle danger in characterizing whole groups as "wicked" or "brutal" or "aggressive," et cetera, or in regarding "the wicked" as a sort of separate species. The transition from "the enemy" to "the wicked" is easy and natural. Then comes the transfer to the adversary of attitudes supposed to be proper toward the wicked, with an accompanying sense not only of guiltlessness but of positive righteousness in sharing the moral-order's condemnation of the wicked. The next step is a zeal to be an instrument for that punishment of the wicked which justice apparently demands, and the next—"righteous war."

Before examining the Biblical material, we need to attempt an analysis of certain concepts fundamental to the discussion of our problem.

Henotheism is "the belief in a special supreme god for each region, race, or nation." Since we may find throughout a large portion of the Old Testament material a henotheistic view, the belief that Yahweh is the "special supreme God" of the Hebrews, and that other peoples have their own gods, it seems desirable to note some of the implications of henotheism with regard to the problem of attitudes toward war.

The god of one tribal or national group has no responsibility for other peoples. Their own gods must care for them. Human

---

[7] Cf. Gilbert, George Holley, *The Bible and Universal Peace*, ch. VI. E.g., speaking of certain writers during the Civil War, "Both poets claim the God of the Bible for their respective armies, but the point to be especially noted is that their thought of him is one with that which was cherished among the Hebrews a thousand years before Christ. He is a man of war, the captain now of the Union Army, and anon of the Confederate; it is he who scatters the enemies and makes them fall.

Bayard Taylor sings to the northern soldiers,
  'God fights with ye,'
and with equal confidence a southern bard exclaims,
  'The God of battles will listen to our cry'" (pp. 158 f.).

lives are therefore not equally valuable in the sight of this god. His own people have a unique significance and worth. The fortunes of his people as a group are his chief concern, and are to be furthered even at the cost of great harm to other groups. When, therefore, economic pressure or ambition for political expansion, or any other cause, makes the territory of another nation seem desirable for his people, the needs or rights of the other group are not a vital consideration to him, and need be no deterrent to the effort to take what is desired. The god therefore uses his power on behalf of his group against the other group, which is logically interpreted as his fighting against the god of the other group.

Victory for his group indicates the superiority of his power over that of the other god.[8] Defeat for his group may be interpreted as an indication either that his power is inferior or that for some reason he has not exerted it to the full. The latter explanation is the one usually resorted to, and it leads to the question why the god is displeased with his people, and the attempt to propitiate him.[9]

[8] Fowler, *The Literature of Ancient Israel*, p. 43, remarks: "The phrase 'my god Ashur giving me the victory' recurs with monotonous uniformity in the records of the Assyrian kings."
It is interesting to compare with Hebrew accounts of victory through Yahweh the following excerpts from King Mesha's inscription on the Moabite Stone: "And I made this high place for Chemosh in Karhoh (?) in (gratitude for) deliverance, because he saved me from all assailants (?) and because he made me see my desire upon all those who hated me. . . . Omri was king of Israel and he afflicted Moab many days, because Chemosh was angry with his land . . . but Chemosh restored it in my days . . . and the king of Israel built Ataroth for himself. And I fought against the city and took it. And I slew all the people; the city (became) a gazing-stock to Chemosh and to Moab. And from there I brought the altar-hearth of Dodoh (?); and I dragged it before Chemosh in Kerioth; . . . Then Chemosh said to me, 'Go and take Nebo against Israel.' So I went by night and fought against it from the break of dawn until noon, and I took it and slew them all—seven thousand men and women and . . . female slaves—for I had devoted it to Ashtar-Chemosh. And the king of Israel had fortified Jahaz, and occupied it while he fought against me. But Chemosh drove him out before me. . . . And at Horonaim dwelt the . . . And Chemosh said to me, 'Go down, fight against Horonaim'; so I went down (and fought against the city many days, and) Chemosh (restored it) in my days . . ."
Kent, *Israel's Historical and Biographical Narratives*, p. 495. For a slightly different translation, cf. Barton, *Archaeology and the Bible* (1925 edition), pp. 421 f.

[9] A case of such propitiation of Chemosh, the god of Moab, occurs in II Kings 3:27. "Then he (Mesha) took his eldest son that should have reigned in his stead, and offered him for a burnt-offering upon the wall. And there was great wrath (of Chemosh) against Israel: and they departed from him, and returned to their own land."

Refinement of the conception of the quality of the god's relationship to his own people may progress indefinitely far, without assuming that any of these attitudes extend to others beyond the pale of the special group.

Development toward a monotheistic idea naturally comes for each group, if at all, through a broadening of the conception of the dominion of its own particular god.[10] It is possible that the extension of different elements in his relationship to men may not proceed at the same rate. For instance, the god's control of other nations or enforcement of ethical requirements upon them may be conceived before he is thought of as vitally caring for other nations. When a god has complete control but not impartial interest, he no longer fights against other gods for the sake of his people; he now manipulates other nations, like pawns, in the interest of "his people." At this stage, victory in battle is easily understood. Defeat gains a new significance; it can no longer mean lack of power in the god, and it is not now due merely to the god's failure to exert himself fully against the enemy, but is explained as his actually fighting on the side of the enemy. Since his purposes, however, are still centered in the welfare of his own people, defeat requires an explanation, and stimulates them, as in the former stage of thought, to try to discover wherein they have offended the god.

In introducing a discussion of God's attitudes toward war, it may be desirable also to distinguish several different aspects of the conception "god of war."

A god of war might be a being whose sole function is to motivate or control or participate in war, and who would therefore lose all significance for mankind if war were eradicated from life, or, on the other hand, a being, possessing other more essential characteristics, who fights only upon occasion, as a corollary of his championship of some cause or group involved in war. We

[10] It will be seen later that in Israel this growth from henotheism to monotheism is not the result of philosophical speculation, but, rather, the result of the conception of Yahweh as the supreme embodiment of righteousness, and a Being capable of enforcing His moral standards. Since the fundamental ethical requirements would not naturally be limited to just one people, such a God would pass ethical judgments upon other nations—and then would punish wickedness wherever He found it. At this point, Yahweh's dominion has been carried beyond that of a henotheistic deity, and we have a "practical monotheism."

CHAPTER II

THE EARLIEST HEBREW LITERATURE

1. Early Poetic Fragments—2. Early Narrative of the Establishment of the Kingdom—3. The Book of the Acts of Solomon—4. Early Laws

EARLY POETIC FRAGMENTS

WAR AND MARCH SONGS FROM BEFORE 1000 B.C.

The fragments of poetry scattered through the narrative of Hebrew history are, as a rule, much older than the writings in which they are now incorporated, and may often be assigned to the very time of the events with which they are associated. Most of these have a bearing upon this investigation.

The Song of Lamech (Gen. 4:23-24) exults in unlimited personal revenge.

In the Song of Miriam (Ex. 15:21) Yahweh[1] Himself has "triumphed gloriously" over the Egyptians. In Exodus 17:16, Yahweh has sworn that He will have war with Amalek from generation to generation. The incantations to the Ark (Num. 10:35-36) anticipate that Yahweh's enemies will be scattered, and that then He will return to the camp of Israel. The list of stations in Numbers 21:14-15 is taken from "The Book of the Wars of Yahweh." The taunt song on the Amorites (Num. 21:27-30) rejoices in the defeat of Sihon and the ravaging of his territory. Yahweh is not explicitly mentioned, but the assumption would be that He had enabled Israel to conquer the Amor-

---

[1] It has seemed wise to follow the custom of most present-day scholars and use the form "Yahweh" (also transliterated by some scholars "Jahveh" or "Jahweh") for the proper name of the God of the Hebrews. Since all Biblical quotations, however, have been taken verbatim from the American Standard Version, the form "Jehovah" (composed of the consonants of "Jahveh" and the vowels of "Adonai") has been retained in *quoted* passages. This variation in form is occasionally rather awkward, but seems, on the whole, a way of avoiding still worse confusion.

ites. In Joshua's appeal to the sun and moon, the day lasts long enough for the Israelites to avenge themselves on their enemies (Josh. 10:12-13).

A longer ancient poem is the Song of Deborah (Judg. 5), a triumphal ode upon the defeat of Sisera. Praise for this victory belongs to Yahweh, who came amid storm and earthquake from the regions where He had formerly most strikingly manifested Himself to His people. To tell of it is to "rehearse the righteous acts of Jehovah." The forces of nature, presumably under His direction, aid the Israelites, the stars in their courses fighting against Sisera, the River Kishon sweeping away the enemy. Meroz is cursed for not coming "to the help of Jehovah against the mighty," while Jael will be signally blessed for treacherously killing the leader of the enemy. The epilogue voices the prayer:

So let all thine enemies perish, O Jehovah:
But let them that love him be as the sun when he goeth forth in his might. (5:31)

The ideas most characteristic of this early poetic material are seen to be that enemies of Israel are enemies of Israel's God, Yahweh; that wars against these enemies are essentially wars waged by Yahweh; and that Yahweh's methods of fighting are to control natural phenomena so as to overwhelm the enemy, and to strengthen His own people in their battling for Him. This is simple henotheism.

PROPHETIC BLESSINGS AND ORACLES BEFORE AND DURING THE EARLY MONARCHY

The Blessing of Noah (Gen. 9:25-27) assumes that Yahweh will respond to the curse upon Canaan. Interestingly enough, however, He will bless not only Shem, the ancestor of the Israelites, but also Japheth, apparently at Shem's expense.[2]

The Blessing of Jacob (Gen. 49:2-27) contains some oracles that seem to come from the period of the Judges, some from the

---

[2] The poem comes clearly from some time after the subjugation of the Canaanites by the invading Hebrews, but the identity of "Japheth" is a moot point, and so the date is uncertain.

early monarchy, and apparently one (on Joseph) from the divided kingdom.

The fierce anger of Simeon and Levi and their "weapons of violence" are objects of imprecation (49:5-7). The summum bonum for any tribe, however, is the defeat of enemies and resultant dominion over other peoples. For Judah,

> Thy hand shall be on the neck of thine enemies,
> Thy father's sons shall bow down before thee. (49:8; cf. vss. 9-10)

For Joseph, also, to be able to resist his persecutors and have his arms made strong by the Mighty One of Jacob (vss. 23-24) is the main point in a most comprehensive blessing. Benjamin, too, shall "devour the prey" and "divide the spoil" (vs. 27).

The Oracles of Balaam evidently come from the time of Saul and David. It is probable that the oracles in Numbers 24 are older than the ones in chapter 23, and that the former were finally incorporated in J, and the latter in E.[3] We shall, however, treat them together.

It is significant that here Yahweh is using a non-Israelite as His mouthpiece.

Balaam's oracles are wholly a glorification of Israel, which gains special force from the idea that these words of blessing and admiration were spoken under divine compulsion, when the seer had been brought for the purpose of uttering a curse (23:7-8, 20).

In this nation, Yahweh "hath not beheld iniquity," and so "Jehovah his God is with him" (23:21; cf. vs. 10). The result of Yahweh's presence and favor will be a countless posterity (23:10), prospering in every conceivable way (e.g., 24:5-7). The chief feature of this prosperity is the destruction of all national enemies. Israel will be a lion to his foes, eating the prey, and drinking the blood of the slain (23:24). Or, strong as a wild ox,

> He shall eat up the nations his adversaries,
> And shall break their bones in pieces,
> And smite them through with his arrows. (24:8)

[3] Cf. Brightman, *Sources of the Hexateuch*, pp. 104, 176.

Under a great king to come, he will possess the territory of neighboring hostile nations—Moab, Edom, Amalek, and the Kenites (24:17-22).

POETRY FROM ca. 1000 B. C. TO 910 B. C.

A few of the poetic fragments from the period extending from David's time through the reign of Jeroboam I are not relevant here, but most of them need to be noted.

In the song of the women about David's victories, the ground of his popularity is that he has slain "ten thousands" to Saul's thousands (I Sam. 18:7). Sheba's war cry rings out the summons, "Every man to his tents, O Israel!" (II Sam. 20:1) David's lament over Saul and Jonathan celebrates, among the other virtues of "the mighty" who have fallen, the fact that their weapons were never wont to return empty "from the blood of the slain, from the fat of the mighty" (II Sam. 1:22).

In the Blessing of Moses (Deut. 33), we have the reflection of a somewhat later stage in the interrelations of the Hebrew tribes than the Blessing of Jacob depicts. It seems to have been written in the northern kingdom, probably during the reign of Jeroboam I, though scholars are not fully agreed as to the date.

The main point for our purpose is to note that again the dominant element in almost every blessing is the idea of victory over enemies. For example, for Levi Yahweh is to

Smite through the loins of them that rise up against him,
And of them that hate him, that they rise not again. (vs. 11)

Joseph will have mighty horns with which "he shall push the peoples all of them, even the ends of the earth" (vs. 17; cf. vss. 7*d*, 20, 22, 23*d*, 29). Even the beautiful assurance by a later writer,

The eternal God is thy dwelling-place,
And underneath are the everlasting arms,

is followed immediately by

And he thrust out the enemy from before thee,
And said, Destroy. (vs. 27)

The poems from this period, then, as a rule breathe the air of the battlefield and count victory in war the greatest good for any group. To this time belongs also the lost collection of poems called "The Book of the Wars of Yahweh"—a title that hardly seems strange after what we have seen of the nature of early Hebrew poetry.

Early Narrative of the Establishment of the Kingdom

It was probably during the reign of Solomon that someone who had been in intimate touch with the circumstances of David's rise and reign undertook to write a narrative of the events that had led to the establishment of the monarchy, and to trace its history during the first two reigns, with special attention to those personal and political phases of David's career which the writer seems to have known at first hand.

The stories about the fortunes of the ark of Yahweh in the premonarchic days of the Philistine oppression, with which the narrative of the kingdom is introduced, shed an interesting light upon certain aspects of a rather early conception of Yahweh.

Yahweh is a God of mysterious and terrifying power, which He exercises in unaccountable ways. He is not identified with the ark, but this chest is a tangible evidence of His covenant with Israel, and a sort of focus of His mysterious energy.

The magical power of the ark seems to be exercised or not according to Yahweh's will on the occasion—rather, the ark in itself has no power, but Yahweh is extremely jealous for its dignity, since it represents His covenant, and hence, where the ark is, Yahweh usually gives some dreadful and unmistakable manifestation of His presence.

This is what the Israelites are counting upon when, after a defeat which can only mean Yahweh's failure to fight for them, they think to insure His aid by bringing the ark into battle (I Sam. 4:3). The Philistines share the Israelites' belief in the potency of the ark and are appalled at the presence of "these mighty gods" (I Sam. 4:7-8), yet this spurs them to such desperate effort that they win the battle, slaying many Israelites and capturing the ark (4:9-11a).

The unthinkable has happened—Yahweh has not even saved the ark itself! Soon, however, the stage is set for a dramatic manifestation of His presence with it. The ark of Yahweh is deposited in the house of Dagon! Yahweh must now show His superior power, and accordingly Dagon's votaries twice find the image of their god lying vanquished and helpless before the ark (I Sam. 5:3-4).

Now that He has begun to act in defense of His ark, Yahweh will not stop until it is restored to Israel. From city to city the dismayed Philistines carry it, and wherever it rests the hand of Yahweh is heavy upon the city; He smites many of its people with death and the rest with tumors (I Sam. 5:6-12). In despair, the Philistines decide at length to try to placate this havoc-working God by sending back His ark, accompanied by golden images of the tumors and mice with which He has plagued them. They are convinced that Yahweh is indeed the author of their disasters when the cows that draw the ark are mysteriously driven away from their calves, straight toward Israel (I Sam. 6:9-12).

At the border Israelite village of Beth-shemesh, the astonished people give themselves over to rejoicing and sacrificing to Yahweh, but in their ardor they offend Him by looking into the ark, and its sanctity is defended at the expense of over fifty thousand lives (I Sam. 6:19-20).

It is not strange that the people of Beth-shemesh think it expedient to pass on to another village the intensive presence of this "holy" God, whose power is not yet joined to good-will and moral responsibility, but rather to caprice and jealousy and terrifying destructiveness.

In the remainder of the early narrative of the kingdom, the ark figures less prominently, yet Yahweh's power is several times associated with it. When the ark is being brought up to Jerusalem, Yahweh terrifies the people by smiting the rashly helpful Uzzah (II Sam. 6:6-9). After testing Yahweh's mood by depositing the ark temporarily with Obed-Edom, the Gittite, David takes courage and finally brings it safely into Jerusalem (II Sam. 6:11-15).

Though Yahweh's presence is not confined to the immediate

vicinity of the ark, it does seem to be limited, in David's thought, to the territory of His own people, for he pleads with Saul: ". . . they have driven me out this day that I should not cleave unto the inheritance of Jehovah, saying, Go, serve other gods. Now therefore, let not my blood fall to the earth away from the presence of Jehovah" (I Sam. 26:19b-20a).

Yahweh's attitude toward Israel in this early narrative is on the whole one of benevolence. He bids Samuel anoint a man as "prince" to save His people from the Philistines, and each step in the institution of the monarchy seems to meet with His favor. (Cf. I Sam. 9:16; 10:1; 11:15.) A similar idea as to Yahweh's gracious purpose to rescue His people from their oppressors is expressed by Abner when he is trying to alienate the elders of Israel from the house of Saul and win their allegiance for David (II Sam. 3:18).[4]

Yahweh can be depended upon to reward virtuous conduct, such as David's sparing the life of Saul, His anointed (I Sam. 26:23-24), and the reverential treatment of Saul's body by the men of Jabesh-Gilead (II Sam. 2:5-6).

Yahweh's special favor toward David is frequently mentioned. When Saul's jealous hatred is deepening, we learn that "Saul was afraid of David, because Jehovah was with him, and was departed from Saul" (I Sam. 18:12) and David's success in winning the hand of Michal further demonstrates His favor (18:28a; cf. 16:18b). Abigail expresses her conviction that Yahweh purposes only good for David (I Sam. 25:28-29). After his capture of Jerusalem, "David waxed greater and greater; for Jehovah, the God of hosts, was with him" (II Sam. 5:10).

Yahweh's favor toward David would naturally be shown largely by His cutting off David's enemies. In Abigail's speech referred to above, He is to sling out their souls "as from the hollow of a sling" (I Sam. 25:29b). Jonathan looks forward to the time "when Jehovah hath cut off the enemies of David every one from the face of the earth" (I Sam. 20:15b). The smiting of the Philistines at Baal-perazim means to David: "Jehovah

[4] Cf. II Sam. 5:3, 12. The idea of the "loving kindness of Yahweh" occurs in an interesting context in I Sam. 20:14-15a and II Sam. 9:3.

hath broken mine enemies before me" (II Sam. 5:20), and after the defeat of Absalom, Ahimaaz pleads with Joab: "Let me now run, and bear the king tidings, how that Jehovah hath avenged him of his enemies" (II Sam. 18:19; cf. vss. 28b, 31).

The enemies of the Hebrews are called the enemies of Yahweh in David's message accompanying his presents to the elders of Judah (I Sam. 30:26).

Throughout the narrative, the Israelites regard Yahweh as the determiner of events, particularly of the outcome of battle. It seems rather, though, because they consider Him the strongest power, than because they believe Him to be the one power, in control of other nations. If Yahweh wills to fight for His people—as He presumably does unless some sin of theirs has displeased Him—victory is sure, because He can defeat all other gods as He defeated Dagon in Dagon's own house (I Sam. 5:1-4). When Yahweh does fight for Israel, His might is sufficient, without dependence upon a large army (cf. I Sam. 14:6, 12, 23). Yahweh's jealousy for His own honor, His inseparable attachment to Israel, and His ability to save His own chosen ones from any power confronting them, are well expressed in David's words before his conflict with Goliath (I Sam. 17:36-37, 45-47; cf. I Sam. 19:5; 30:23).[5, 6]

Yahweh's foreknowledge of events is placed at the disposal of the king through the casting of lots, or the priestly oracle of the ephod, to the end that the military tactics or the personal policies of David may be wisely directed. The narrative includes frequent decisions based on these oracular responses. (Cf. I Sam. 23:2-5, 10-12; 30:8; II Sam. 2:1; 5:19, 24.)

From the discussion so far, it is clearly evident that, whatever may be displeasing to Yahweh, war is not. The killing of the nation's foes is foretold by Him and is accomplished through His aid again and again.[7]

[5] Some of the main elements in this account of the fight with Goliath are clearly unhistorical (cf. II Sam. 21:19), but possibly the story had crept into a narrative written even as soon as this after David's time.

[6] Further aspects of Yahweh's control of events are seen in II Sam. 15:25-26, 31; 17:14; 16:10b-12.

[7] Against this background, it is interesting to note that the violation of an oath, or the slaying of Yahweh's anointed, either priests or king, or the cultic sin of "eating with the blood," would be evil in Yahweh's eyes. (Cf. I Sam. 14:38-39a; 22:17b; 26:8-11a; and 14:33.)

Entirely distinct from national blood-guiltiness, or the slaying of individuals in war, which is praiseworthy, is the personal blood-guiltiness which is to be

18   The God of the Old Testament in Relation to War

Many passages in which Yahweh is not mentioned help to reveal the militant spirit and the brutal methods of warfare that were a part of the national experience, in the midst of which Yahweh moved as the God of Israel.

The ignominious terms proposed by Nahash, the Ammonite, to the men of Jabesh-Gilead are that all their right eyes be put out (I Sam. 11:2), but Saul wreaks vengeance by thoroughly smiting the Ammonites in battle (11:11).

The cause of David's rapidly growing popularity is:

Saul hath slain his thousands,
And David his ten thousands.   (I Sam. 18:7)

Saul takes revenge for the assistance innocently given to David by the priests of Nob by slaying "both men and women, children and sucklings, and oxen and asses and sheep" (I Sam. 22:18-19).

In his raids against enemy tribes while he was a vassal of Achish of Gath, David "saved neither man nor woman alive" (I Sam. 27:8-9; cf. 30:17).

When the king of Ammon died, "David said, I will show kindness unto Hanum the son of Nahash, as his father showed kindness unto me. So David sent by his servants to comfort him concerning his father" (II Sam. 10:2). But this ill-starred attempt at international condolence resulted only in shameful treatment of David's messengers, and a brutal revenge of Israel upon Ammon (II Sam. 11:1; 12:31).

An interestingly humane touch is introduced in David's readiness to spare Ittai of Gath from sharing his misfortunes during Absalom's rebellion. Possibly its purpose is to test Ittai's loyalty, but it seems worth noting (II Sam. 15:19-20).

This early narrative of the kingdom is most objectively written, with little apparent effort at religious teaching. The greater number of passages shedding light on the conception of Yahweh have had to be taken from the speeches of the actors in

avoided. (Cf. I Sam. 25:26, 32-34; II Sam. 3:28-29, 39b; I Kings 2:5.) Churlish conduct like that of Nabal toward David is punished by Yahweh (I Sam. 25:38-39a) and David's adultery with Bath-sheba and arrangement for the death of Uriah are unequivocally condemned by Yahweh (II Sam. 11:27b; 12:1a, 7-10, 13a).

the history, since the historian adds remarkably few interpretative comments.

The portrayal of Yahweh thus obtained, however, seems a consistent one. He is the God of Israel, and of Israel alone. Certain moral requirements are imposed upon His people, and certain others which are superstitious—or "religious" according to the ideas of that day—rather than ethical. None of these moral or religious ideas in any way suggests a doubt as to the rightness of warfare. The battles with which this story deals are almost entirely for the defense of territory or national dignity or the throne of David, but there is no indication that under more favorable circumstances warfare would be limited to the defense of something. A later writer inserts in this narrative an account of David's conquest of neighboring nations (II Sam. 8); it is impossible to be sure why we do not have this in the earlier document.

The God of Israel bestows favor upon David and, in less degree, upon certain other outstanding individuals, to the end that His people may profit. To the people at large, however, His mysterious and terrifying manifestations of power must be fully as striking as His gracious acts.

Yet, though He may occasionally punish His own people, the full force of His power to smite is felt only by their enemies, and the gods of their enemies. When need arises, He is "Yahweh of hosts, the God of the armies of Israel," and at all times His presence and His care are for Israel alone. The author of this narrative was, like his contemporaries, a henotheist.

The Book of the Acts of Solomon

The basis of the narrative of Solomon's reign in I Kings 3-11 is a certain Book of the Acts of Solomon, mentioned in I Kings 11:41, and probably written not long after the close of his reign. The original chronicle has doubtless been much altered and elaborated, but for our present purpose we may deal with these chapters as they now stand.

"Jehovah, the God of Israel" (e.g., 8:23, 26) is a God dwelling in heaven (8:27, 30, etc.), yet peculiarly present in the

Temple (6:11-13; 9:3). The people of Israel have been separated from among all the peoples of the earth to be Yahweh's inheritance (8:53), but their blessing from Him depends upon their obedience to His will (9:4-9).

Yahweh in His lovingkindness blesses those whose conduct is pleasing to Him, putting David's enemies finally "under the soles of his feet" (5:3), and giving him a son to succeed him on the throne (3:6). He offers Solomon the latter blessing, also, if he is as faithful to Him (9:4-5). Pleased with Solomon's request for "an understanding heart to judge thy people," rather than for long life, riches, or the life of his enemies (3:9-11), Yahweh gives him the wisdom asked for, and riches and honor besides (3:13; cf. 10:10, 23-25). As a result of this divine favor, Solomon rules over a great empire, with subject nations bringing tribute to him (4:21). Peace is the consequence of his dominion over all his neighbors (4:24-25). When he offends Yahweh by building sanctuaries for the gods of his foreign wives, several of the vassal nations are enabled by Yahweh to revolt (11:14, 23) and Yahweh's intention to rend the kingdom of Israel itself is revealed to Jeroboam through a prophet (11:31-33).

Some rather different relations of Solomon with other peoples should be noted. He makes an alliance with the Pharaoh of Egypt, sealed by marriage with his daughter (3:1), and later marries many other foreign women, with the unfortunate result that "his heart was not perfect with Jehovah his God, as was the heart of David, his father" (11:4; cf. 11:5-8). Solomon has an alliance and a friendly exchange of favors with Hiram of Tyre (5:1-12), and amicable relations with the Queen of Sheba (10:1-10, 13). A skilled craftsman from Tyre is the most prominent workman on the Temple (7:13-14). There is, of course, no necessity for treating the remnant of the Canaanites with the consideration shown in Solomon's dealings with important nations, so these people are made bondservants (9:20-21).

In Solomon's prayer at the dedication of the Temple, which is doubtless largely the work of a later day, we have many petitions that are significant for this study. Since defeat in battle (8:33, 46) or drought, famine, pestilence, blasting, insect plagues, or siege by an enemy (8:35,37) are all supposedly

The Earliest Hebrew Literature

traceable to Yahweh's displeasure on account of sin, the appeal for forgiveness when His people supplicate Him in the Temple carries with it the expectation of restoration to prosperity. The only petition at all surprising is that Yahweh will grant the prayer of "the foreigner, that is not of thy people Israel, when he shall come out of a far country for thy name's sake . . . that all the peoples of the earth may know thy name, to fear thee, as doth thy people Israel, and that they may know that this house which I have built is called by thy name" (8:41-43). It is interesting that this universalistic passage is immediately followed by a supplication for victory in battle (8:44-45).

According to this narrative of the reign of Solomon, then, Yahweh appears to permit friendly relations with other nations as long as they contribute to Israel's prestige and do not weaken loyalty to Him, but He has no care for other nations such as He has for Israel, and favor to Israel involves dominion over others. Freedom for the people of Edom and Zobah is not an end in itself, but merely a means of punishing Solomon. To Israel, and particularly to its kings, David and Solomon, Yahweh is gracious while they show wholehearted devotion to His purposes for the nation.

Early Laws

Perhaps it was during the reign of Solomon that the ethical and cultic laws which had been gradually wrought out of the group experience of the Hebrews were codified in the so-called Book of the Covenant (Ex. 20:22 to 23:19) and the decalogue of Exodus 34:10-26.

The God of these early laws has two great concerns—the undivided loyalty of His people, to be evidenced by their proper observance of His cult and avoidance of the idolatrous practices of their neighbors, and, secondly, the equitable ordering of the relations between individuals in the Hebrew community.

The Hebrews are to be "holy men" unto God (Ex. 22:31). His relations with other nations are touched upon only briefly. The deliverance of the Hebrews from Egypt is to be commemorated in the feast of unleavened bread (Ex. 23:15; 34:18), and the men need not fear to leave their homes to appear before the God of Israel at the feasts three times a year, "for I will cast out nations before thee, and enlarge thy borders: neither shall any man desire thy land, when thou goest up to appear before Jehovah thy God three times in the year" (Ex. 34:24).

God's attitude toward the Hebrews is essentially gracious (Ex. 20:24*b*), but depends upon their conduct. They must worship no other god, "for Jehovah, whose name is Jealous, is a jealous God" (Ex. 34:14; cf. 20:23). He discriminates between the righteous and the wicked within the nation. He hears the cry of the oppressed poor, for He is "gracious" (Ex. 22:27); against those who afflict the helpless "my wrath shall wax hot, and I will kill you with the sword" (Ex. 22:24). The effort to protect the weaker members of the community includes precautions against oppression of a sojourner, "for ye know the heart of a sojourner, seeing ye were sojourners in the land of Egypt" (Ex. 23:9; cf. 22:21; 23:12). Only a Hebrew servant, however, need be set free in the seventh year (21:2).

The "lex talionis," making revenge exactly proportionate to the injury, requires: "Thou shalt give life for life . . ." (Ex. 21:23; cf. 21:12, 14). The death penalty is to be inflicted also for such crimes as smiting or cursing father or mother (21:15, 17), stealing a man (21:16), practicing sorcery (22:18), and sacrificing unto any other god than Yahweh (22:20). In each case, the killing of the guilty person is clearly intended to protect the lives of other members of the community.

The requirement that one who finds a straying animal belonging to his "enemy" should bring it to the owner, or that one should release a fallen animal of "him that hateth" him, is worth noting, though this deals only with relations between members of the community.

In short, God is here interested in the Hebrews only (with the exception of sojourners), but the stress is on His ideal for their faithfulness to Him and justice toward one another, rather than on their relations with other nations.

CHAPTER III

NARRATIVES FROM THE NINTH AND EIGHTH CENTURIES

1. Narratives from the Ninth Century Now Incorporated in the Books of Kings—2. The J Document—3. The E Document

NARRATIVES FROM THE NINTH CENTURY NOW INCORPORATED IN THE BOOKS OF KINGS

ELIJAH STORIES

The cycle of stories about Elijah in I Kings 17-19 and 21 probably took shape not long after his death, sometime after 850 B.C. In these stories, Yahweh, through His prophet, is in constant conflict with the wicked queen and king who seduce His people to worship the Tyrian Baal (ch. 18) and who disregard His requirements of social justice (ch. 21).

He is a God of mighty power, manifested chiefly through natural phenomena. There will be no rain for a period of years, except through Elijah's word (17:1), and Yahweh sends fire from heaven to reveal Himself in Elijah's contest with the prophets of Baal on Mount Carmel (18:36-39). His miraculous control of nature is shown also in His care for His prophet during the drought (17:4, 14).

We strike a unique conception, not inherent in other parts of the story, when Yahweh reveals Himself to Elijah on Mount Horeb not in the wind, earthquake, or fire, but in the "still small voice" (19:12).

Elijah's methods against his religious enemies are illuminating. Apparently in accordance with Yahweh's will, he slays all the prophets of Baal, defeated in the trial by fire on Mount Carmel. The very same treatment had been used by Jezebel toward the prophets of Yahweh (18:4, 13) and, of course, had been considered most dreadful. The slaughter of a hostile religious group is evidently not offensive to Yahweh, provided His worshipers are the victorious party.

Similarly, bloodshed is anticipated in His commission to Elijah on Mount Horeb (just after the revelation through the "still small voice"!). He must anoint Hazael and Jehu and Elisha—"and it shall come to pass, that him that escapeth from the sword of Hazael shall Jehu slay; and him that escapeth from the sword of Jehu shall Elisha slay"—yet Yahweh will leave alive the seven thousand that have not worshipped Baal (19:15-18).

ELISHA STORIES

In II Kings 2; 4:1 to 6:23; 8:1-6; and 13:14-21 we have a group of stories about the prophet Elisha, in which he appears as the miracle-working "man of God," a more benign figure than we shall find in the document that we are to consider after this one.

Yahweh is here characterized chiefly by His power to intervene in the ordinary course of events and work marvels through His prophet. Elisha's situations and judgments of moral values determine whether this power shall be drawn upon for beneficent purposes—healing the waters of Jericho (II K. 2:20-22), feeding "the sons of the prophets" by counteracting the poison in the pottage or multiplying loaves (4:38-44), reviving the dead son of the Shunammite woman (4:32-37), and restoring to health the Syrian leper (5:8-14)—or for destructive purposes, bringing bears to tear forty-two disrespectful boys (2:24), and causing Naaman's leprosy to come upon Gehazi (5:27). Elisha's unfailing clairvoyance with regard to the movements of the Syrian army is a great military asset (6:8-12), but Yahweh's participation in the wars between Syria and Israel is made still clearer when, on his deathbed, Elisha directs Joash how to shoot "Jehovah's arrow of victory over Syria," as an omen of triumph, and then to smite on the ground, an act which proves to be the token of the number of Israel's coming victories. The man of God is "wroth with him" for not striking enough times so that Israel could wholly "consume" Syria (13:15-19). Elisha seems always certain as to how Yahweh will act; the other "sons of the prophets" are less intimately in touch with the divine activity; they do know the day when Elijah is to be taken away

(2:3,5) but they do not fully grasp the fact of his translation into heaven, fearing "lest the Spirit of Jehovah hath taken him up, and cast him upon some mountain, or into some valley" (2:16).

Protected by divine power, the man of God need fear nothing. A great host of the Syrians, sent to take him, is helpless—the mountain is "full of horses and chariots of fire round about Elisha," and in answer to his prayer Yahweh smites the enemies with temporary blindness (6:14-18).

The rest of this incident is interesting for us. Elisha leads the blinded soldiers into Samaria, then has Yahweh restore their sight, and bids the king of Israel to feed and liberate the captives, instead of smiting them. This generous treatment has the encouraging result that, for a while at least, "the bands of Syria came no more into the land of Israel" (6:19-23), but it is just an isolated anecdote and has no influence upon the conduct of the succeeding wars.

Elisha's readiness to heal the Syrian captain of leprosy may likewise indicate a kindly spirit toward a representative of the nation usually hostile to Israel, though this act of mercy seems to be largely the result of a desire to demonstrate the presence and power of a great "prophet in Israel" (5:8). Yahweh may be acceptably worshipped by the grateful Syrian, but Elisha offers no protest against Naaman's request for two loads of the earth of Yahweh's land in order to be able to worship Him in Syria. Yahweh must be bound closely to the land where His people dwell.

In the collection of Elisha stories, we have found war in the background, with clear evidence of Yahweh's steady partisanship for Israel, but with two instances of generous treatment of enemies. Yahweh is a national God, dwelling only in the land of the Israelites. Actual battle is not the theme of these tales—rather, the wonder-working power of the man of God.

HISTORY OF THE RISE AND FALL OF THE DYNASTY OF OMRI

In I Kings 20 and 22 and II Kings 3; 6:24 to 7:20; 8:7-15; and 9:1-10:28, we seem to have abstracts from a history of the rise and fall of the dynasty of Omri, written in Israel during the reign of Jehu.[1]

The parts of this history that have been preserved deal mainly with the wars of Ahab and Jehoram. Though on the whole the story is objectively told, with little interpretation of events, Yahweh is clearly the giver of victory in battle.

Because the Syrians think that Yahweh is a god of the hills, and can conquer only there, He will defeat them in the valley also (I K. 20:28-29). Again, when the allied armies of Israel, Judah, and Edom are in sore straits during a campaign against Moab, Yahweh brings water into the valley—"and this is but a light thing in the sight of Jehovah: he will also deliver the Moabites into your hand. And ye shall smite every fortified city, and every choice city, and shall fell every good tree, and stop all fountains of water, and mar every good piece of land with stones" (II K. 3:18-19). This devastation of Moab, divinely ordered through the prophet Elisha, is thoroughly accomplished (3:23-25). On another occasion, however, a comparatively harmless method is used against an enemy; when Samaria is being besieged, the Lord makes the Syrians "hear a noise of chariots, and a noise of horses, even the noise of a great host" and flee in terror (7:6-7).

The grimness of the conception of Yahweh is indicated in this document largely by the offices performed by His prophets. When Ahab shows mercy to his royal captive, Ben-hadad of Syria, and makes a covenant with him instead of slaying him, this new kind of international policy is vigorously denounced by a prophet: "Thus saith Jehovah, Because thou hast let go out of thy hand the man whom I had devoted to destruction, therefore thy life shall go for his life, and thy people for his people" (I K. 20:42). To "entice Ahab, that he may go up and fall at Ramoth-Gilead," Yahweh, according to the true prophet Micaiah, sends a lying spirit into all the other prophets to promise success (I K. 22:19-23). Finally, Elisha subtly instigates Hazael to murder his sick master, Ben-hadad of Syria, and in Israel more boldly rouses Jehu to bloody revolt. By making a wholesale slaughter of the descendants of Ahab and the worshipers of Baal, Jehu adequately demonstrates his "zeal for Jehovah" (II K. 9:1 to 10:28).

[1] Cf. Bewer, J. A., *The Literature of the Old Testament*, pp. 52-59.

Narratives from the Ninth and Eighth Centuries

In the fragments of this early historical writing that we have been examining, Yahweh appears as a national God who devotes to destruction individuals or groups within or without the nation whenever they weaken His people's loyalty to Him or oppose His plans for their welfare, and who accomplishes His purposes either directly or through prophets who in their zeal for Him have absolutely no regard for human life as such.

The J Document

About 850 B.C., when Elijah was startling King Ahab and the people of the northern kingdom with his vigorous and dramatic efforts to revive loyalty to Yahweh, conditions in the southern kingdom under the comparatively "good" King Jehoshaphat seemed to call for less drastic treatment. A prophetic spirit, or a group of like-minded writers, living in Judah at this time, sought to awaken deeper loyalty to Yahweh by writing down old stories of Israel's history from the earliest times, giving them an impressive setting in a view of Yahweh's dealings with mankind from the creation on.[2]

The Yahweh of the J document is to some extent interested in humanity as such. This is particularly true in Genesis, for events in this part of the story do not usually involve situations where one nation is pitted against another, with Yahweh's care and help limited to just one side.

Long before the division into the separate nations of J's day, "then began *men* to call upon the name of Jehovah" (Gen. 4:26). Representatives of various peoples included in the Genesis story either worship Yahweh or find that He is accessible, or at least voluntarily recognize Him as the source of the prosperity of certain individuals.[3]

[2] Narratives similar to the J strand of the Hexateuch are found in Judges. It is difficult to determine whether they were included in the original J document; this may possibly have carried events even up to the writer's own day.
The document is called J because of its use of the divine name "Yahweh" throughout the narrative. (Cf. "E")

[3] Nimrod is "a mighty hunter before Jehovah" (Gen. 10:9); Hagar the Egyptian learns that "Jehovah hath heard thy affliction" (Gen. 16:11); Lot, the father of Moab and Ammon, is saved by men who are angels of Yahweh

It is significant that among Yahweh's frequent promises of the land and a great and blessed posterity, two to Abraham (Gen. 12:3; 18:18),[4] one to Isaac (Gen. 26:4),[4] and one to Jacob (Gen. 28:14), include the idea that "in thee shall all the nations of the earth be blessed." Whether this carries with it any of the altruistic flavor suggested by the English rendering, or merely means that all other peoples shall be so impressed by the greatness of this family that when uttering a blessing they shall say, for instance, "Be thou like Abraham!" it at least indicates the breadth of J's horizon and gives some slight sense of the oneness of humanity.

Moreover, in Yahweh's dealings with Pharaoh and his people, though He sends plagues upon the Egyptians, as we shall note in another connection, the characteristic conception in J is that Pharaoh hardened his heart (Ex. 7:14; 8:15, 32; 9:7, 34), rather than that Yahweh hardened Pharaoh's heart.[5]

Yahweh's presence and power are not limited to any one territory. He is in control of nature everywhere,[6] and theophanies or other special communications from Him occur in a great variety of places.[7]

(Gen. 19:12-22); Laban and Bethuel recognize Yahweh's determining guidance in the proceedings leading to Rebekah's betrothal (Gen. 24:50-51), and Laban appeals to Him at Galeed (Gen. 31:53 a); Abimelech concludes that Yahweh is with Isaac (Gen. 26:28); Potiphar, the Egyptian, recognizes Yahweh as the cause of Joseph's prosperity (Gen. 39:3), and so, apparently, does the Egyptian prison-keeper (Gen. 39:23); and Potiphar's house is blessed by Yahweh—though, to be sure, for Joseph's sake. In Numbers 22:18, we find that Balaam is constrained to obey Yahweh, *his* God.

[4] Gen. 18:18 and 26:4 occur in passages usually considered to be later additions to J. (Cf. Brightman, *The Sources of the Hexateuch*, pp. 44, 53.)

[5] The exception to this (Ex. 10:1) is probably the work of a redactor. Cf. Brightman, *op. cit.*, p. 87.

[6] Yahweh can curse the ground for Adam and for Cain (Gen. 3:17; 4:11-12); He can destroy all living beings by a flood (Gen. 6-8, *passim*), and then can agree never to curse the ground or smite all creatures again, and guarantee the regular succession of seasons (Gen. 8:21, 22); He can give superior crops to Isaac during his sojourn among the Philistines (Gen. 26:12-14); He can cause and then remove the disasters in Egypt (Ex. 7-12, *passim*), control the waters of the Red Sea (Ex. 14:21b), and provide manna and quails for the Israelites in the wilderness (Ex. 16:4; Num. 11:31). These striking manifestations, when explained, are traced to Yahweh's manipulation of the winds (Ex. 10:13b, 19a; 14:21b; Num. 11:31a).

[7] For instance, in the Garden of Eden (Gen. 3); in the land of Shinar (Gen. 11:5-9); in Haran (Gen. 12:1-4 a; 31:3); at numerous places in Canaan, including Mamre (Gen. 18:1-15), Beth-el (Gen. 28:13-16), and Peniel (Gen. 32:24-31); in the land of Midian (Ex. 3:2 ff.); in Egypt (Ex. 7-12, *passim*); upon Mount Sinai (Ex. 19, *passim*, and 24:9-11), and elsewhere in the wilderness.

Even while observing the Yahwist's consciousness of humanity and his breadth of view, certain qualifications of his tolerance have had to be noted, and it is certainly far from true that all nations appear as of equal worth to the Yahweh of the J document.

In Genesis, Yahweh's partiality for Abraham, Isaac, and Jacob appears primarily in His special revelations of Himself, and His often repeated promise, foreshadowed in Noah's curse and blessings (Gen. 9:25-27), to give them and their seed the land of Canaan and to make of their descendants an innumerable people.[8] Without regard to what other tribes and nations were then occupying it, His people would eventually possess it all. Though Genesis holds no story of armed conquest of territory, the conquest when it does occur seems in J simply the inevitable realization of a divine purpose revealed again and again to the patriarchs, and hence something which is a priori justifiable and even natural.

After Genesis, Yahweh's people are in more perilous circumstances, and He appears as more actively partisan. Seven plagues are first threatened through Moses and then sent by Yahweh upon the Egyptians (Ex. 7-12, *passim*). In connection with several of these, Yahweh's discrimination between the Israelites and the Egyptians is especially stressed (Ex. 8:22-23a; 9:4, 25b-26; 11:4-5a, 6-7; 12:23). At the Red Sea, Yahweh drowns the Egyptians in the returning waters, after letting His own people through dry-shod (Ex. 14:27b, 28b). At a later time, in pleading with Yahweh, Moses well expresses the idea of Israel's separation from all other peoples (Ex. 33:15b-16). Finally, Yahweh makes a covenant to do unexampled marvels on behalf of His people when they invade the land of Canaan (Ex. 34:10).

This leads to the inquiry, to what extent Yahweh appears as a fighting God.

At the Red Sea, Moses tells the terrified Israelites, "Jehovah

---

[8] The promise, which in its entirety contains three ideas—the land, a great and blessed nation, and "in thee shall all the families of the earth be blessed" —is given, in whole or in part, to Abraham six times in J, Gen. 12:1-3, 12:6-7 a, (13:14-17), (15:7), 15:18 a, (18:18); to Isaac twice, Gen. 26:2-4, and 26:23-24; to Jacob once, Gen. 28:13-15; and to Moses four times, Ex. 3:8, 33:1-3 a, (34:11), (34:24), and is referred to in a number of other places. The passages in parenthesis are probably later additions to the J document; cf. Brightman, *op. cit.*

will fight for you, and ye shall hold your peace" (Ex. 14:14). In other words, in this case Yahweh will "fight" with other means than armies to gain their deliverance from the Egyptians, and later the cry of the Egyptians in their discomfiture shows that they are convinced of Yahweh's fighting (Ex. 14:25b).

Yahweh makes a covenant to drive out before Israel all the nations in Canaan (Ex. 34:10-11), and when the tribes are uncertain whether to brave the dangers of the invasion, the words of the two courageous spies express a firm belief in Yahweh's partisan effort (Num. 14:8-9). Yahweh "delivers up" the people of Arad after the Israelites vow to Him that in that event they will destroy these people utterly (Num. 21:1-3). Joshua, by Jericho, sees "a man over against him with his sword drawn in his hand," who proclaims himself "prince of the host of Jehovah" (Josh. 5:13-14a), and the military successes of the tribes of Judah and Joseph are interpreted in Judges 1 as indicating, "Jehovah was with them."

Constant struggle between tribal or national groups seems presupposed as part of the natural order of things. Out of the Semites' nomadic experience, with its intertribal struggle for existence in the grudging desert, and out of the death grapple of world empires and the continual internecine warfare of the East-Mediterranean nations, the authors of the J document inherited the conviction that enemies were inevitable and the conquest and domination of other peoples the only real security.[9]

The indications in J as to Yahweh's evaluation of human life seem at first not quite consistent. Allowance must be made for two controlling conceptions. The whole group is treated according to the desert of an outstanding individual or individuals,[10] and, secondly, the conception of the worth of human life as such does not affect any dealings with national enemies. The Egyptians and the Canaanites, in time of conflict with them, may be

[9] Ishmael's "hand shall be against every man, and every man's hand against him; and he shall dwell over against all his brethren" (Gen. 16:12). The blessing upon Rebekah from her family is: "Our sister, be thou the mother of thousands of ten thousands, and let thy seed possess the gate of those that hate them" (Gen. 24:60). Cf. also Gen. 25:23; 27:29, 40; Ex. 1:10.

[10] Noah's righteousness saves his whole family (Gen. 7:1); ten righteous, if they could have been found, would have saved Sodom (Gen. 18:32) (though Abraham's intercession for Sodom is "viewed by most as a later addition," cf. Brightman, *op. cit.*, p. 44, and Bewer, *The Literature of the Old Testament*, p. 73); Lot's family are, or could have been, rescued with him (Gen. 19:12); Pharaoh's stubborn disobedience brings calamities upon his whole people.

wiped out without compunction, usually by Yahweh's own agency. Similarly, when unlimited wickedness has made human beings enemies to Yahweh's original purposes, there is no deterrent consideration of the value of human life to prevent Yahweh from drowning all mankind, except righteous Noah and his family (Gen. 6:5-8; 7:22-23).

Yet, in spite of these attitudes, we have the story of Abel's blood crying from the ground to Yahweh (Gen. 4:8b-12); we have Yahweh's protection of Cain's life by means of a special tribal mark (Gen. 4:13-15); and we find Yahweh ready to meet half-way every intercession of Abraham for the deliverance of Sodom (Gen. 18:22-23).[11] The mark of Cain, however, can hardly be called an indication of the value of human life in general, since it is a warning of seven-fold revenge upon slayers of members of that tribe. The intercession for Sodom is for the sake of the righteous who would be involved in the punishment of the city, while the rightness of Yahweh's slaying the wicked goes unquestioned. In short, the story of the murder of Abel is the only clear protest of Yahweh against bloodshed—and that case is the killing of a brother, with no implications as to the attitude toward wholesale killing of other peoples.

The Yahweh of J seems to have had some great benevolent purpose for all humanity when He created them, and later a special purpose for Abraham and his seed. But all the way along men block His design by "wickedness" and disobedience, and in quite anthropopathic wrath and confusion He strikes back at them with some form of destruction. Though there is a steady current of gracious providence making for the ultimate greatness and prosperity of Yahweh's people, the surface waters of history are considerably ruffled by a sort of divine trial-and-error method, with intervals when Yahweh feels thwarted and baffled by the failure of mankind or of the chosen nation to cooperate with His purpose.

Yahweh's lovingkindness and compassionate providence are revealed in such familiar incidents as His making coats of skins for the ejected Adam and Eve (Gen 3:21), His giving the sign

[11] Judah's plea to his brethren to save Joseph's life is scarcely relevant, since the reason urged for sparing him is: "for he is our brother, our flesh" (Gen. 37:27).

to Cain (Gen. 4:14-15), His saving Noah and his family (Gen. 7:1), the revelation of his angel to Hagar (Gen. 16:7-14), His readiness to stretch justice in the direction of mercy in dealing with Sodom (Gen. 18:22-23), and His insistent rescue of the procrastinating Lot (Gen. 19:16). Jacob speaks of "all the lovingkindness, and . . . all the truth, which thou hast showed unto thy servant" (Gen. 32:10). Yahweh reveals to Moses His compassion for His people who are suffering and sorrowing in Egypt (Ex. 3:7-8). He leads them during their perilous journey by the pillar of cloud and of fire (Ex. 13:21-22); He shows Moses a tree that will make the bitter waters sweet (Ex. 15:25a); He provides manna (Ex. 16:4-5), and, later, quails (Num. 11:31). When asked by Moses for a sight of His glory, He responds, "I will make all my goodness pass before thee" (Ex. 33:19), and His character as proclaimed to Moses is: "Jehovah, Jehovah, a God merciful and gracious, slow to anger, and abundant in lovingkindness and truth; keeping lovingkindness for thousands, forgiving iniquity and transgression and sin; and that will by no means clear the guilty, visiting the iniquity of the fathers upon the children, and upon the children's children, upon the third and upon the fourth generation" (Ex. 34:6-7).[12]

This Yahweh, though often so graciously kind to those who seem to merit it, is severe in His punishment of wickedness, as has already appeared in several instances. (Cf. Gen. 3; 4:8b-12; 6-8, *passim;* 18: 20-21; 19: 23-28; 38: 7, 10; Ex. 7-12, *passim.*) As for His own people, the penalty for their continued grumbling is a terrible plague at the very moment of their feasting on the quails (Num. 11:33), while their lack of faith and courage at the border of Canaan brings a threat of smiting and disinheritance, with the final decision that their children shall enter the promised land, while they themselves shall be condemned to forty years of wandering, until their dead bodies shall be consumed in the wilderness (Num. 14:31-33).

The sense of divine bewilderment and confusion of issues in all this comes mainly from the frequent ascription of anger to Yahweh, an anger which is usually appeased by destruction. (Cf. Ex. 4:13-14, 24; 5:3; 19:21-22; Num. 11:10, 33; 22:22a-

---

[12] Though this passage is probably a redaction, the conception of Yahweh's character seems in harmony with the set of J passages under discussion here.

33b; 25:4). Occasionally, Yahweh's destructive activity is halted by intercession, as when the plagues in Egypt are stopped upon Moses' entreaty (Ex. 8:12-13, 30-31; 9:33; 10:18-19).[13]

The complete, almost magic, power attributed to the human word spoken in blessing or cursing contributes to the impression of uncertainty as to the free activity of a consistently benevolent divine purpose. As a matter of fact, however, the patriarchal blessings and curses seem to reflect Yahweh's ultimate designs, and they serve in this story as an effective device for suggesting the prosperity and power for the favored ones which is actually realized in the dénouement.

Certain other strange elements have crept into the portrayal of Yahweh's character. His jealousy is the cause of the dispersion of peoples and difference of language (Gen. 11:1-9),[14] and He is represented as instigating Moses to lie to liberate the Israelites (Ex. 3:18).[15]

The J document recounts several other incidents that have significance in the discussion of war attitudes, even though Yahweh is not mentioned.

Scorn for neighboring nations could not be more bitingly expressed than in the story of the incestuous birth of Moab and Ammon (Gen. 19:36-38).

The idea that all other peoples in Canaan must be either wiped out or else reduced to slavery before the Israelites can safely reside in the land is tersely given in their reply to the Gibeonites: "Peradventure ye dwell among us; and how shall we make a covenant with you?" (Josh. 9:7)

In contrast to this story from the fiercely militant period of the conquest, we have in the patriarchal legends the story of Isaac's relations with Abimelech, a non-Hebrew (Gen. 26:

[13] The original J document probably did not contain the interview now recounted in Num. 14: 11-21 (cf. Brightman, *op. cit.*, p. 101) where Yahweh threatens to smite His people "with the pestilence, and disinherit them," and offers to make of Moses "a nation greater and mightier than they," but Moses finally obtains a pardon for them by a clever *argumentum ad hominem*.

[14] The Tower of Babel story seems to imply that a united mankind is capable of unlimited achievement, but Yahweh fears the possible encroachment upon His own sovereignty and so frustrates man's designs before it is too late.

[15] Though the scheme is aimed throughout at securing a chance to run away, Moses is to go to Pharaoh on the pretext of the Israelites' desire to sacrifice to Yahweh in the wilderness, where the sacrificial animals will not offend the Egyptians.

1-33). In the incident of the deception regarding Rebekah, Isaac is pictured with less dignity and honor than Abimelech; in the succeeding events, though, where he repeatedly suffers injustice at the hands of the men of Gerar, Isaac becomes a hero —yet a strange kind of hero for ancient times. He persistently refuses to stand up for his rights! Through patience, forbearance, and self-sacrifice for the sake of peace, he finally attains Abimelech's recognition of his superior favor with Yahweh, and a covenant assuring mutual safety, after which Abimelech departs from him ''in peace.''

Moreover, the portrayal of Esau's treatment of Jacob is remarkable. That he possesses a real grievance against Jacob is made unquestionably clear by the narrative of Jacob's treacherous acquisition of their father's blessing, and is doubly evidenced by the trepidation with which Jacob approaches Esau's vicinity upon his return from Haran. Yet Esau, the ancestor of the kingdom of Edom, is represented as the soul of magnanimity, and responds to Jacob's peace-offering: ''I have enough, my brother; let that which thou hast be thine'' (Gen. 33:9).

To summarize, the thought of the J document moves to some extent among mankind as such, and certain incidents suggest a noteworthy tolerance or even generosity toward non-Israelites. [Yet whenever the situation involves an apparent conflict between the advantage of this people and that of some other nation, Yahweh is clearly the God of Abraham and his seed. The God who created mankind fights for just one people. He may temporarily become angry with them and smite them to punish their refractory conduct, but after all it is their welfare as a people that alone concerns Him supremely.] The Yahweh of J is essentially a national God, in spite of the occasional glimpses of a broader conception.

EARLY (J?) MATERIAL IN JUDGES

Possibly the J document extended beyond the Hexateuch, including most of the hero tales that now serve as the basis of the book of Judges,[16] and even incorporating the early narrative

---

[16] For a list of these early passages in Judges, cf. Bewer, J. A., *The Literature of the Old Testament*, p. 68, footnote, or Moore, G. F., *The Book of Judges*, Polychrome Edition, *passim*.

of the establishment of the kingdom, which we have already examined.

The early hero stories in Judges are full of battle and bloodshed, but Yahweh's part in it all appears only incidentally.

Ehud's "message from God" to the king of Moab is delivered by thrusting him through with a sword (3:20-22).

Victory in battle is interpreted as the work of Yahweh, as when Ehud tells his followers: "Jehovah hath delivered your enemies the Moabites into your hand" (3:28; cf. 8:7; 11:9; 12:3). The Song of Deborah, incorporated in this document (5:2-31a), deals with the same idea in more detail, as we have already seen.

The coming of "the Spirit of Yahweh" upon a hero endows him with special physical strength for great exploits, as in the case of Jephthah (11:29) and Samson (13:25; 14:6, 19; 15:14).

Most prominence of all is given to the burly, bloody, simpleminded Samson, whose birth and consecration as "a Nazirite unto God" are foretold by "the angel of Jehovah" (13:2-14) and whose special blessing from Yahweh is emphasized (13:24). Samson's desire to marry the Philistine woman of Timnah was "of Jehovah; for he sought an occasion against the Philistines" (14:4). Yahweh cleaved the earth in Lehi so that the thirsty hero might be refreshed after felling a thousand men (15:18-19). However, after the cutting of Samson's hair, "Jehovah was departed from him" (16:20c), though the keeping of the Nazirite vow had apparently been a purely mechanical thing, certainly with no ethical significance. In the end, Yahweh answers Samson's prayer for strength "that I may be at once avenged of the Philistines for my two eyes," and thus enables him to slay more Philistines at his death than during his life (16:28-30).

In the account of the migration of the Danites, might makes right, whether against a helpless Ephraimite whose idols and priest they want to steal (18:18-26), or against a non-Israelitish city, "quiet and secure," with "no deliverer," whose territory they want to steal with Yahweh's favor (18:27-28).

Thus, in these ancient tales we seem to have a purely henotheistic idea of Yahweh, a God who gives victory to the Israelite heroes endowed with physical might by His Spirit. The lack of any very clear conception of Yahweh's ethical requirements is noteworthy, also. Patriotism is here enough—and in the case of Samson, we find very little even of that. To have killed a great many Philistines, whatever the motive, suffices to make him a hero.

The E Document

Probably about 750 B.C., during the reign of Jeroboam II,[17] at about the time when Amos was delivering his sermons of doom, another man, or group of men, was trying to convey a message of prophetic insight to the northern kingdom, through the channel of history. E, or the Elohist,[18] by tracing the course of Israel's relations with Yahweh from the time of the patriarch Abraham on,[19] tried to teach the people of his day how Yahweh had in the past directed Israel's history through chosen prophets, what sort of God Yahweh was, and what He required of His people.

The E document lacks most of the broader human touches found in J, partly because E's story begins with God's promise to Abram, and hence does not include the period when God dealt with men as men and not as Israelites or non-Israelites.

All of God's dealings with non-Israelites naturally center in their relations with Abraham and his seed. His communication with Abimelech in a dream is for the sake of Sarah's safety. Though God recognizes Abimelech's innocence, still he and his family cannot be completely restored without the intercession of Abraham, the "prophet" (Gen. 20:6-7, 17). The Egyptian midwives are favored by God and rewarded with households, because they "feared God, and did not as the king of Egypt commanded them, but saved the men-children (of the Hebrews) alive" (Ex. 1:17). In E, it is Yahweh who hardens Pharaoh's heart (Ex. 10:20, 27), as the result of which he and his people

---

[17] Cf. the summary of conditions during this reign, opening the discussion of Amos.

[18] So called because, in contrast to J, this document uses the divine name "Elohim" until the revelation of "Yahweh" to Moses.

[19] The point to which E brought the history is a question—through Joshua's time, or Samuel's, or up to his own day? We shall here treat the E strand of the Hexateuch first, and then add a brief discussion of material similar to E in the books dealing with a later period.

are plagued. As in J, we find Balaam blessing Israel in obedience to Yahweh's word communicated directly to him. In short, the God whose main interest is in the Hebrews can, when need arises, direct the thought or conduct of non-Israelites who have dealings with them.

As in J, these outsiders sometimes avow their recognition of God's presence with Abraham and his seed.[20]

God's promise of the land of Canaan and a blessed posterity for His chosen ones is reiterated frequently in E, as in J. Though the idea that "in thy seed shall all the nations of the earth be blessed" (Gen. 22:18a) occurs only once, in a passage attributed to the editor of JE,[21] and immediately following the assertion, "thy seed shall possess the gate of his enemies" (Gen. 22:17b), the other two parts of the promise are given, either separately or together, many times.[22] The result of the conception that their God has promised them this land is the conviction that it does actually belong to them, and the sooner they occupy their "inheritance," the better. (Cf. Josh. 13:1, 7; 18:2-3.)

Because Ishmael, too, is Abraham's seed, God will make him a great nation (Gen. 21:13, 18).

God's care for these chosen ones for whom He purposes such a great future appears throughout the story. Jacob shows Rachel and Leah, "Thus God hath taken away the cattle of your father, and given them to me" (Gen. 30:9). When Jacob and all his household are journeying to Beth-el, "a terror of God was upon the cities that were round about them, and they did not pursue after the sons of Jacob" (Gen. 35:5). Joseph's apparent misfortunes, culminating in his position of prestige in Egypt, are a part of God's providence for the children of Israel (Gen. 45:7-8a). When blessing Joseph and his sons, Jacob describes Him as "the God before whom my fathers Abraham and Isaac

---

[20] Abimelech and Phicol seek a covenant with Abraham because "God is with thee in all that thou doest" (Gen. 21:22 b); Pharaoh, much impressed with Joseph, asks his servants, "Can we find such a one as this, a man in whom the spirit of God is?" (Gen. 41:38); and Rahab tells the spies, "I know that Jehovah hath given you the land" (Josh. 2:9 a).

[21] Cf. Brightman, *The Sources of the Hexateuch*, pp. 126 f.

[22] Given by God to Abram in Gen. 15:5, 16, and 21:12 b; and to Jacob in Gen. 46:3-4; to Joseph by Jacob in Gen. 48:21; to his brethren by the dying Joseph in Gen. 50:24; to the people by Yahweh before leaving Sinai in Ex. 23:23-30; to Joshua in Deut. 31:23; and to Moses on Pisgah in Deut. 34:1b-4.

did walk, the God who hath fed me all my life long unto this day, the angel who hath redeemed me from all evil" (Gen. 48:15-16a). God, at this point revealed as "Yahweh," is sensitive to the need of His oppressed people in Egypt, and through Moses will rescue them (Ex. 3:9-10). This marvelous deliverance is a theme frequently touched in E, as in most of the other Old Testament writings, and the most impressive introduction that could be found for the Decalogue is: "I am Jehovah thy God, who brought thee out of the land of Egypt, out of the house of bondage" (Ex. 20:2). During the wilderness journey, He provides the thirsty people with water out of the rock at Horeb (Ex. 17:6a), and later He promises to give them every blessing, and victory over all their enemies, if they will obey the angel that He sends before them. (Ex. 23:20-22, 25-27.)

The idea that Yahweh will be an enemy to their enemies, involved in the complete conception of His care for Israel, is, of course, stressed whenever their enemies figure prominently in the story. Though, as previously noted, Yahweh "hardens Pharaoh's heart" Himself, He visits that offender and his people with five dreadful plagues. Not content with liberating the Israelites from Egypt, Yahweh instigates them to borrow jewels and raiment from the Egyptians, to the end that they may steal them (Ex. 12:35-36). At the Red Sea, the divine protector of the Israelites takes off the chariot wheels of the Egyptians (Ex. 14:25a), and the Song of Miriam, incorporated in E, rings out the summons exultantly:

Sing ye to Jehovah, for he hath triumphed gloriously,
The horse and his rider hath he thrown into the sea. (Ex. 15:21) [23]

After the conquest of the East Jordan country, when the Israelites' further invasion of a territory occupied by other peoples is blocked by the River Jordan, the "Lord of all the earth" piles up the waters to let them pass (Josh. 3:10a, 11-13).

When we come to the conquest of Canaan as narrated in Joshua, we find much JE material upon whose analysis scholars disagree considerably.[24] The fact that this material is here

[23] Yahweh's vow to have eternal war with Amalek (Ex. 17:16) and the invocation to the ark (Num. 10:35-36) are also included in E.
[24] Cf. Brightman, *op. cit.*, pp. 184 f.

Narratives from the Ninth and Eighth Centuries 39

treated with the later document, E, gives to J less of "frightfulness," and to E comparatively more, than may be deserved.

The conquered cities of Jericho and Ai are by Yahweh's command to be "devoted," completely destroyed, "both young and old, and ox, and sheep, and ass, with the edge of the sword" (Josh. 6:16-17, 21, 26; 8:1-2, 7-8, 18, 24-26).

Yahweh plays the leading part in the defeat of the kings of South Canaan, killing more men with great hailstones than the children of Israel slay with the sword (Josh. 10:10-11). To consummate the victory, Yahweh, according to E's interpretation of an old poetic fragment, "hearkened unto the voice of a man" and caused the sun and moon to stand still until the nation had avenged themselves on their enemies. (Cf. Josh. 10: 19-21.)

It is through Yahweh, also, that Joshua defeats the kings of North Canaan. "And Jehovah said unto Joshua, Be not afraid because of them; for to-morrow at this time will I deliver them up all slain before Israel: thou shalt hock their horses, and burn their chariots with fire" (Josh. 11:6).

Against such a background, the Decalogue's prohibition of killing (Ex. 20:13) will be seen to have no bearing upon the conduct of warfare.

Throughout the account of the conquest, the wholesale slaying of man, woman, and child needs no justification. These people are in the land, and Yahweh purposes that the Israelites shall have it. That is enough. The idea of the iniquity of the Amorites, suggested in connection with God's first promise to Abram (Gen. 15:16) as a supplementary reason for wiping them out, is not utilized again, though of course their worship is viewed as a seduction to apostasy (Josh. 24, *passim*).

Though Yahweh is thus usually found fighting for His people, there are occasions, as in J, when His fierce anger is turned upon them because of their grumbling or disobedience or some other disloyalty.

After the people's apostasy in connection with the golden calf, the way to regain Yahweh's favor is to have those who are on His side slay the others (Ex. 32:37). The next day, when Moses makes confession of their sin and implores Yahweh: "Yet now, if thou wilt forgive their sin . . . ; and if not, blot me, I pray thee, out of thy book which thou hast written," Yahweh refuses to accept his vicarious atonement (Ex. 32:32-35; cf. 33:3b). Later, anger at the people's murmuring brings the fire of Yahweh upon them (Num. 11:1-2). The rebellion of Aaron and Miriam against Moses kindles Yahweh's anger against them (Num. 12:9-10a). To allay His anger after the people have worshipped Baal-peor, all the apostates must be slain (Num. 25:3b, 5). In several cases, Moses seems to have more forbearance than Yahweh, and it is his intercession which prevents a still more serious or prolonged punishment.[25]

Yahweh, assuredly, does not feel that he must "not kill." A perusal of these instances of Yahweh's uncompromising methods in the punishment of wrongdoing seems to justify Joshua's warning to the people: "Ye cannot serve Jehovah; for he is a holy God; he is a jealous God; he will not forgive your transgressions nor your sins. If ye forsake Jehovah, and serve foreign gods, then he will turn and do you evil, and consume you, after that he hath done you good" (Josh. 24:19-20). It is little wonder that back at Sinai, when Yahweh was manifesting His presence in thunders and lightnings and a thick cloud of smoke (Ex. 19:16-19; 20:18), the people trembled and besought Moses: "Let not God speak with us, lest we die" (Ex. 20: 19b).

As in the J document, we have in E a number of passages which are of interest for this discussion, even though they do not explicitly shed light upon the character of Yahweh.

The stipulations of kindness and fair dealing in the covenant between Abraham and Abimelech are noteworthy (Gen. 21:23), but of greatest significance are the two attempts of the Israelites, under Moses, to pass peacefully through kingdoms that lie across their route to Canaan (Num. 20:14-17; 21:22). In neither case does the method prove successful; Edom's armed refusal necessitates a detour, while Sihon's similar response leads to pitched battles, in which "Israel smote with the edge of the sword," and so "possessed his land from Arnon unto the Jabbok" (Num. 21: 24). The effort to avoid war is remarkable, but the account would hardly encourage reliance upon any substitute.

[25] For other cases of Yahweh's anger, or of relentless punishment where "anger" is not actually mentioned, see Josh. 7: 7-26; Num. 14: 22-24, 42-45; 16: 29-32; 21: 6.

Few Old Testament stories offer a more seductive snare to religious commentators than the story of how Israel profits by Rahab's cowardly treachery to her own city. Her protection of the Hebrew spies is clearly prompted by no idea of the intrinsic value of human life, nor by allegiance to Yahweh, but purely by her cunning purpose to save herself and her family amid the coming slaughter of her neighbors.

In summary, we have found that the E document portrays a national God. Though Yahweh visits His people with dire punishment when His anger is aroused by the disobedience or faithlessness of individuals or of the nation, His whole concern is for Abraham and his seed, and for their sakes He fells any people that may consciously or unconsciously impede their progress toward the high destiny set for them.

E (?) MATERIAL IN JUDGES AND SAMUEL

The author of the E document, or another writer representing the same school of thought, worked over earlier stories of the "judges," adding a few others,[26] and recounted events connected with the establishment of the monarchy from a point of view very different from that of the early narrative written soon after David's time.[27]

On account of the Israelites' apostasy after Joshua's death (Judg. 2:13), "the anger of Jehovah was kindled against Israel" (2:20), and He did not drive out "the nations that Joshua left," but let them stay in the land to test Israel's loyalty to Him (2:21, 23; 3:4). Later, however, when His people were grievously subjugated by their neighbors and cried unto Yahweh (6:7; 10:10), if they became duly penitent and turned loyally to Him again "his soul was grieved for the misery of Israel" (10:16).[28]

As in the earlier stories in Judges, Yahweh takes part in warfare. According to the E story of the defeat of Sisera (4:6-22),

[26] Cf. Bewer, *op. cit.*, p. 82, and Moore, G. F., *The Book of Judges*, Polychrome Edition, *passim*.

[27] Cf. Smith, H. P., *International Critical Commentary* on *Samuel*, pp. xviii, xxiii-xxvi, and Bewer, *op. cit.*, pp. 82-84.

[28] We shall later find similar ideas developed with still greater consistency in the Deuteronomistic framework of Judges.

the battle at the River Kishon and Sisera's death by the hand of a woman are planned by "Jehovah, the God of Israel," as revealed through the prophetess Deborah (4:6-9). Yahweh goes out before Barak's army, and Himself discomfits "Sisera, and all his chariots, and all his host, with the edge of the sword before Barak" (4:14-15). Gideon's three hundred men shout, "The sword of Jehovah and of Gideon" (7:20c), but by requiring such a small army Yahweh has taken precautions against much dependence upon any might but His. He proves His adequacy to overwhelm the Midianites when He sets "every man's sword against his fellow, and against all the host" (7:22; cf. 8:3). After Jephthah's vow to offer as a burnt-offering whosoever first comes out of his house to meet him upon his return, Yahweh delivers the Ammonites into Jephthah's hand. (It seems as though the deduction *post hoc, ergo propter hoc* would not here be a fallacy.)

In Samuel, too, Yahweh requires fierce revenge upon the enemies of His people. "Thus saith Jehovah of hosts, I have marked that which Amalek did to Israel, how he set himself against him in the way, when he came up out of Egypt. Now go and smite Amalek, and utterly destroy all that they have, and spare them not; but slay both man and woman, infant and suckling, ox and sheep, camel and ass" (I Sam. 15:2-3). When Saul spares King Agag and the best of the animals, his disobedience to Yahweh's command of complete extermination brings his rejection by Yahweh (15:17-23; cf. 28:17-18). Having delivered the divine message to Saul, Samuel himself "hewed Agag in pieces before Jehovah in Gilgal" (15:33b).

According to Professor Moore, we should assign to the editor who combined the J and E documents a passage which contains the clearest possible statement of the henotheistic view implicit in all this material. Jephthah, trying to ward off an invasion by the Ammonites, says in his message to them: "So now Jehovah, the God of Israel, hath dispossessed the Amorites from before his people Israel, and shouldest thou possess them? Wilt not thou possess that which Chemosh thy god giveth thee to possess? So whomsoever Jehovah our God hath dispossessed from before us, them will we possess" (11:23-24).

E's idea is that Yahweh wants to rule His people directly, through prophets or "judges" raised up when occasion demands, not through any established monarchy, with hereditary kingship. Wherever possible, this is brought out in Judges (8:22-23; 9:8-15; 9:50-57).

In Samuel, however, the material of the story is even better suited to emphasize this conception. When the people ask Samuel to give them a king, Yahweh tells him: "They have not rejected thee, but they have rejected me, that I should not be king over them" (I Sam. 8:7; cf. 10:17-19). Yahweh will let them have a king, but they are warned that he and his successors will oppress them so that they will cry out to Him, "and Jehovah will not answer you in that day" (I Sam. 8:9-18). This is in marked contrast to the earlier view of the king as one given by Yahweh to save His people from their enemies (e.g., I Sam. 9:16); the pessimism of the E writer reflects his experience of the dynastic chaos during the period following the reign of Jeroboam II, which convinced Hosea, also, of the impotence and sinfulness of kingship. The tragic end of the first king of Israel accorded well with this author's view (I Sam. 28:19-20; 31:1-6).

In this E material, we have pure henotheism, and the situations in the narrative frequently require the national God to fight for His people. If they qualify by loyalty to Him, victory can be won through His power, but Saul after his rejection by Yahweh would, of course, be defeated by the enemy.

CHAPTER IV

PRE-EXILIC PROPHETS

1. Amos—2. Hosea—3. Isaiah—4. Micah—5. The Deuteronomists—6. Zephaniah, Nahum, and Habakkuk—7. Jeremiah

Amos

Under Jeroboam II (*ca.* 783-743 B.C.) the kingdom of Israel enjoyed greater material prosperity and more extended political dominion than at any other time during the period of the divided kingdom. Its most annoying enemy, Syria, was engrossed in the effort to ward off the danger from the rising power of Assyria, and Israel was left free to expand to the east and south. These conditions resulted in a deepened feeling of national security and an opportunity for the leisure classes to become completely absorbed in the superficial pleasures of a luxurious and corrupt society. The "masses" became the helpless victims of the heartless greed and injustice of the "classes." Religion touched the social plague spots not at all, for it had become merely a lavish cultic show for a God who was supposedly bound to the fortunes of His people too closely to risk punishing them.

Up from the southern steppes where he watched his flocks came the austere shepherd Amos, into the markets of the northern cities—and he returned to Tekoa to meditate on Yahweh's relation to all that he had seen of Israel's tainted, hollow life. He looked beyond the borders of Israel and Judah, to their hostile and ruthless neighbors, and still farther to where Assyria was looming ever more threateningly upon the horizon. Then back he came into the cities of Israel to thunder his message of denunciation from the God of righteousness.

The Yahweh of Amos has a direct relation to other nations, independent of His relation to Israel.[1]

[1] Probably the expansion of trade and travel at this time contributed to the possibility of such a conception.

To be sure, he has dealt with Israel in a uniquely intimate way. In recalling His former mercies to this people, which they have met only with a base ingratitude that deepens the blackness of their present sin, Yahweh reminds them that He destroyed the mighty Amorite before them and led Israel in to possess his land (2:9-10). Elsewhere He avers a special nearness to Israel in the past, but only to show that special privilege justifies more rigorous judgment. "You only have I known of all the families of the earth: therefore I will visit upon you all your iniquities" (3:2).

After all, Yahweh has been directing the history of other nations, too—even of Israel's enemies—and Israel's vaunted uniqueness is but a flimsy thing, rendered meaningless by the nation's sin. "Are ye not as the children of the Ethiopians unto me, O children of Israel? saith Jehovah. Have not I brought up Israel out of the land of Egypt, and the Philistines from Caphtor, and the Syrians from Kir? Behold, the eyes of the Lord Jehovah are upon the sinful kingdom, and I will destroy it from off the face of the earth" (9:7-8a).

As other nations have shared with Israel Yahweh's consideration and favor, likewise other nations now share His condemnation and dire punishments. By the same standards—just and humane treatment of fellow-man—Yahweh is judging Israel's neighbors and Israel herself.

For ruthless brutality in war against Gilead, both people and rulers of Damascus and all Syria will be visited with disaster culminating in return to Kir in captivity (1:3-5). For slave trade so inhumanly conducted as practically to annihilate a whole people, Gaza and the other Philistine cities will have people and rulers destroyed, "and the remnant of the Philistines shall perish"(1:6-8). For slave trade accomplished by covenant-breaking, Tyre will meet with calamity (1:9-10). Edom's sin to be punished is merciless warfare against Israel (1:11-12). Ammon's inhuman brutality in aggressive warfare against Gilead will bring upon this people disaster in war and the captivity of its rulers (1:13-15).[2]

Whereas thus far all of the examples of "man's inhumanity

---

[2] For a discussion of these oracles, with the suggestion that those against Tyre and Edom, as well as against Judah, are later interpolations, see Harper, *International Critical Commentary* on *Amos* and *Hosea*, pp. 12-38.

to man" leave room for the discovery of some grievance of Israel against the neighboring nation condemned by Yahweh, His impartial application of His test of righteousness to international relations is demonstrated in the arraignment of Moab. Though Edom has just been shown to be an enemy of Israel, the sin for which Yahweh is to bring upon Moab destruction in battle is that "he burned the bones of the king of Edom into lime" (2:1-3).

Omitting, as the work of an editor, Judah's condemnation for unfaithfulness to the law of Yahweh (2:4-5), we find Israel judged by the same humane standard as the other nations, only more vehemently and picturesquely. For cruel injustice against the poor, resulting from greed, for sexual immorality and heartless revelry even at the altar (2:6-8), Israel will be crushed and rendered utterly helpless (2:13-16).

The international mind of this prophet is indicated also in one of the succeeding oracles, where Ashdod and Egypt are summoned to Samaria to behold the violence and oppression and robbery there, for which "an adversary" will defeat and plunder the guilty ones until only a mangled scrap of Israel can be rescued (3:9-12). Again, in the midst of an arraignment of "them that are at ease in Zion," Amos suggests that they compare their nation with others (6:2).

Though the time was evidently not quite ripe for definitely naming Assyria as the nation that Yahweh would use as His instrument of punishment, Amos is sure of Yahweh's control of the nations and of His preparations to scourge Israel with a certain one. The "adversary" mentioned above is found in another veiled threat: "For, behold, I will raise up against you a nation, O house of Israel, saith Jehovah, the God of hosts; and they shall afflict you from the entrance of Hamath unto the brook of the Arabah" (6:14).

Thus far, we have been investigating Yahweh's relation to the various nations as portrayed by Amos, and we have found an amazing impartiality. In the past, even granting some special intimacy with Israel, Yahweh has guided other nations, too. In the present, He is judging them all uncompromisingly by standards so broadly human that presumably they have all known them, and so might have avoided unrighteousness. If

Israel has had any advantage in the understanding of Yahweh's requirements, her judgment will be correspondingly more severe.

As to Yahweh's attitude toward Israel, though gracious in the past, it is now solely one of condemnation and contemplated punishment.

Yahweh has already chastised the people severely, but all to no avail. Therefore, "prepare to meet thy God, O Israel" (4: 6-12). What Israel considers religious, Yahweh hates; what Israel neglects as of no concern to Him, Yahweh requires (5: 21-24). Any fuller revelation of Yahweh's power and purpose can be only disastrous to such a corrupt people (5: 18-20).

As means of punishment, Yahweh can muster the forces of physical nature against the nation, and afflict it with famine, drought, the blasting of crops, pests of worms or locusts, earthquake and eclipse (4: 6-9; 7: 1-6; 8: 8-9). However, since He holds sway over nations as well as over nature, Yahweh can equally well lash and destroy Israel with disastrous warfare and ignominious captivity. (Cf. 3: 13-15; 4: 1-3; 5: 2-3, 10-12, 16-17, 27; 6: 6-8; 7: 7-9, 17; 8: 1-3; 9: 1-4.)

Yahweh is in complete control; any disaster must be caused by Him. "Shall evil befall a city, and Jehovah hath not done it?" (3: 6b).

There is little hope that the outraged God of righteousness who voices through Amos His threats of doom will relent toward Israel. His "repenting" concerning the proposed scourges of locusts and drought, in response to the prophet's intercession, is followed by further visions and oracles in which destruction for unrighteousness cannot be averted. There are two suggestions of hope that complete reformation of the people may avert the terrible calamity (5: 4-6, 14-15), but throughout most of the book, the assumption seems to be that the nation's corruption is so complete that doom is inevitable.

The concluding promise of restoration from captivity, with marvelous material prosperity, not explicitly contingent upon any moral reformation (9: 11-15), is generally recognized as from another hand.

Amos, then, from the point of view of this study, is extremely significant for portraying a God whose requirements do not include laws or ceremonies revealed only to one nation, but consist solely of common human righteousness and social justice; and a God who enforces these standards internationally and impartially. The original book is entirely free from any nationalistic prejudice.[3]

Only so far, however, does Amos carry us. Yahweh, on the whole, destroys rather than redeems by His punishments, and, in a broader sense than the old nationalistic one, is "God of hosts" (cf. 3:13; 5:14, 15, 16, 27; 6:8, 14), using warfare as one of His chief means of punishing the guilty.

Hosea

After the death of Jeroboam II, the northern kingdom experienced a time of political chaos. One army captain after another was elevated for a brief and ineffectual reign, usually terminated by assassination. Off to the East, the power of Assyria was steadily growing, and Israel was divided into factions over the question whether national safety lay in tribute to Assyria or in resistance to Assyria and reliance upon Egypt. Meanwhile, the social and economic evils which Amos had so forcefully condemned continued unchecked, while the religion of the people at large was essentially an idolatrous and immoral cult. Into this life, the life of his own people, the prophet Hosea attempted to infuse the conception of Yahweh which had come to him out of his own sad experience.

In Hosea, other nations are thought of only in relation to Israel. Yahweh has a special tenderness for this, His people, but there is no explicit comparison of this attitude with His relation to other nations (11:1, 3-4). However, Yahweh must have some control over other nations, if Israel is to be led captive into their territory in accordance with His disciplinary purpose.

The relations with Egypt and Assyria which are inveighed against are not treaties motivated by good-will, leading to international understanding and the prevention of war, but rather

---
[3] Cadbury, *National Ideals in the Old Testament*, p. 110, gives a succinct and stimulating formulation of "the two equations of Amos": "the equality of moral responsibility for all nations in the sight of God, and the equivalence of economic and industrial injustice to the atrocities of war."

"entangling alliances," motivated by fear, and looking toward imminent war with some other nation. "When Ephraim saw his sickness, . . . then went Ephraim to Assyria, and sent to king Jareb: but he is not able to heal you, neither will he cure you of your wound" (5:13). "And Ephraim is like a silly dove, without understanding: they call unto Egypt, they go to Assyria. When they shall go, I will spread my net upon them" (7:11-12a). (Cf. 7:8-9; 8:8-10a; 10:6; 12:1.)

Examining Yahweh's relation to Israel, we find that we still have in Hosea the conception of Yahweh's anger, aroused by His people's unfaithfulness to Him, and the expectation of their severe punishment (8:5; 13:11; 12:14).

Before his tragic experience with his wife and the resulting understanding of Yahweh's character, Hosea apparently felt Yahweh's message to be one of vengeance and rejection, as indicated by the significant names of his three children (1:4, 6b, 9). After this, also, the punitive element is still prominent in his message: "Hear the word of Jehovah, ye children of Israel; for Jehovah hath a controversy with the inhabitants of the land, because there is no truth, nor goodness, nor knowledge of God in the land. . . . Therefore shall the land mourn, and every one that dwelleth therein shall languish" (4:1, 3a). "The people that doth not understand shall be overthrown" (4:14c). "As for Ephraim, their glory shall fly away like a bird: there shall be no birth, and none with child, and no conception. Though they bring up their children, yet will I bereave them, so that not a man shall be left: yea, woe also to them when I depart from them!" (9:11-12) (Cf. 4:6; 5:4, 6, 9; 8:1-3; 10:7-8, 10; 13:12-16.)

Yet, dreadful as are many of these threats, something of the harshness is taken away when we understand Yahweh's attitude. It is not easy for Him to deal these blows. The punishment is wrung from Him by the people's sin, as a means to their redemption—their knowing Him and turning to Him for healing.

"O Ephraim, what shall I do unto thee? . . . for your goodness is as a morning cloud, and as the dew that goeth early away. Therefore have I hewed them by the prophets; I have slain them by the words of my mouth: . . . For I desire goodness, and not sacrifice; and the knowledge of God more than burnt-offerings" (6:4-6). "When I would heal Israel, then is the iniquity of Ephraim uncovered, and the wickedness of Samaria" (7:1a). (Cf. 3:4-5; 5:14-15; 6:1; 7:13; 10:12-13; 11:1-4; 13:4-9.)

. Here speaks a baffled love, which wants to heal and redeem and cherish, but finds itself unable to evoke a response because unable to break through the callousness of unfaithfulness and touch a sensitive spot in the loved one's consciousness.

In most of Hosea's work, Yahweh's purpose is consistent—the redemption of His people. He is struggling to find the method of achieving it. One means after another is grasped at as a possibility. Hence we find many contradictions, since Yahweh has no certainly successful way of dealing with His unfaithful people, but is engaged in an eager search for an effectual method.

Shall He send them back to captivity in Egypt? Yes (8:13b; 9:3, 6a). Yet no—it will not be Egypt again, but Assyria this time (11:5-6). Shall Yahweh punish to the full, as their unfaithfulness seems to deserve? Yes, He will visit upon them dreadful calamities. But no—His divine nature will be revealed to them best if He does not slay them in rage. Anyhow, He can not, for He loves them too much—He can not treat them like Sodom and Gomorrah (11:8-11; 3:1).

Surely in the days to come He will be able to "betroth" Israel to Himself again, this time "in righteousness, and in justice, and in lovingkindness, and in mercies"—even "in faithfulness" (2:18-20; cf. 2:23).

What *shall* Yahweh do to assure their response and return to Him? He must punish—but O Israel, return! And the book ends with pleading and promise, with a sense that such love must eventually prove resistless, and that the restoration which is glimpsed is actually realized. "O Israel, return unto Jehovah thy God; for thou hast fallen by thine iniquity. Take with you words, and return unto Jehovah: say unto him, Take away all iniquity, and accept that which is good: so will we render as bullocks the offering of our lips. Assyria shall not save us; we will not ride upon horses; neither will we say any more to the work of our hands, Ye are our gods, for in thee the fatherless findeth mercy. I will heal their backsliding, I will love them freely; for mine anger is turned away from him. I will be as the dew unto Israel . . ." (14:1-5a).

The book of Hosea, then, makes no contribution toward the conception of an impartial God, nor does it introduce any new ideas as to the possible methods by which He may deal with His people. Its significance lies, rather, in a new portrayal of Yahweh's attitude toward Israel, a love so deep and tender that it will not admit defeat and resort to mere destructive punishment, but instead will find, somehow, a way to redeem Israel. Meanwhile, the prophet Hosea, in his relations with his wife, feels that he is incarnating Yahweh's attitude.

Isaiah

The period of Isaiah's work, 738-700 B.C., witnessed some of the most serious crises ever experienced by the kingdom of Judah. With the Assyrian empire looming ever more threateningly on the horizon; with Judah's sister kingdom to the north eager to throw off the Assyrian yoke, now quietly plotting and now openly rebelling, until the inevitable fruit of such conduct was reaped in defeat and national dissolution; with Judah herself torn by conflicting factions each convinced that escape from a similar disaster could be found only by accepting its own pet policy, whether submission to Assyria or alliance with Egypt and the neighboring nations against Assyria; finally, with faltering kings swayed hither and thither by the waves of popular terror or enthusiasm—throughout these years one figure stood firm, one mind penetrated the tangled problems to the principles underlying them, and one man's faith gripped Yahweh and the spiritual world as the only effective reality. To Isaiah of Jerusalem fell the task of proclaiming to a callous and selfish and bewildered generation the requirements of a God of ethical holiness and world-wide sovereignty, and holding before that generation as its one hope of salvation the way of humble obedience, combined with utter faith in His power and His willingness to respond.

The national crises that furnished pivotal points for Isaiah's message were the Syro-Ephraimitic war against Judah in 735-4, with its terrifying but finally ineffectual siege of Jerusalem; the capture of Samaria and exile of the northern kingdom in 722; continual pressure upon Judah to join Egypt and Philistia in revolt against Assyria, to which King Hezekiah finally yielded;

the resulting devastating invasion of Judah and siege of Jerusalem by Sennacherib in 701, culminating in the dramatic and mysterious withdrawal of the besieging army.

Upon such varied situations, as well as upon the social and religious depravity which called for his denunciation in the periods that intervened, Isaiah directed the force of his oratory.

In adapting his ideas to changing historical situations, Isaiah shifted his emphasis so frequently that now doom and now salvation appears to be Yahweh's purpose for His people.

When Jerusalem was not being besieged, the prophet concerned himself chiefly with the indictment of his people for their social and political and religious wrongdoing, and the pronouncement of Yahweh's condemnation and imminent punishment.

Looking back upon his commissioning, from the vantage point of discouraging prophetic experience, Isaiah feels that Yahweh's answer to his question, "Lord, how long?" must have been: "Until cities be waste without inhabitant, and houses without man, and the land become utterly waste, and Jehovah have removed men far away, and the forsaken places be many in the midst of the land" (6:11-12). Early in his prophetic ministry, he sees in the distance "a day of Jehovah of hosts upon all that is proud and haughty" and warns the people to hide "from before the terror of Jehovah" (2:10-12). (Cf. 3:8, 16-26; 5:8-9, 13-16.) Apparent security is only a delusion: "And the strong shall be as tow, and his work as a spark; and they shall both burn together, and none shall quench them" (1:31).

The passages just quoted probably come from the period between 738 and 735,[4] but after the Syro-Ephraimitic war has passed over, the prophet has to revert to similar threats of doom. As though in amazement at the people's inability to profit by their narrow escape, he complains that they "have not turned unto him that smote them, neither have they sought Jehovah of hosts" (9:13). The future seems to hold only horror; "Through the wrath of Jehovah of hosts is the land burnt up; and the people are as the fuel of fire; no man spareth his brother" (9:19; cf. 9:16-17, 20-21). "And what will ye do in the day of visitation, and in the desolation which shall come

[4] Cf. Bewer, *The Literature of the Old Testament*, footnote, p. 117.

from far? to whom will ye flee for help? and where will ye leave your glory? They shall only bow down under the prisoners, and shall fall under the slain. For all this his anger is not turned away, but his hand is stretched out still" (10:3-4; cf. 5:25; 28:2).

During the period shortly before the crisis of 701, the prophet's message is still mainly a mighty threat (22:5-8). With no realization that Yahweh alone is directing the eventualities of war, the frightened people have recourse to every available material means of protection (22:9-11). Since they have not listened when Yahweh has tried to point out to them the way to rest and refreshing, "by men of strange lips and with another tongue will he speak to this people" (28:11-12; cf. 28:17-19, 21-22; 29:3). Jerusalem "shall be visited of Jehovah of hosts with thunder, and with earthquake, and great noise, with whirlwind and tempest, and the flame of a devouring fire," and with a multitude of hostile nations (29:6-7).

Many of these threats of punishment sound as though nothing but unmitigated destruction awaited Judah, but at some points the redemptive purpose behind the chastisement is made more explicit.

"Therefore saith the Lord, Jehovah of hosts, the Mighty One of Israel, Ah, I will ease me of mine adversaries, and avenge me of mine enemies; and I will turn my hand upon thee, and thoroughly purge away thy dross, and will take away all thy tin; and I will restore thy judges as at the first, and thy counsellors as at the beginning; afterward thou shalt be called The city of righteousness, a faithful town" (1:24-26). Only a remnant will survive the coming calamities, but this chastened remnant will have learned to depend wholly upon Yahweh (10:20-23). In one of the prophet's latest utterances, Yahweh further reveals His beneficent purpose, which, however, is capable of being frustrated by the people's rebellious disobedience. "Come now, and let us reason together, saith Jehovah: though your sins be as scarlet, they shall be as white as snow; though they be red like crimson, they shall be as wool. If ye be willing and obedient, ye shall eat the good of the land: but if ye refuse and rebel, ye shall be devoured with the sword; for the mouth of Jehovah hath spoken it" (1:18-20).

Some of the passages noted in this discussion of Yahweh's

relationship to His own people have implied His sovereignty over more than one nation. Elsewhere, Isaiah stresses the fact that Yahweh has complete control of all nations, using them as His instruments, or rejecting them if they prove unfit for His purpose.

"And it shall come to pass in that day, that Jehovah will hiss for the fly that is in the uttermost part of the rivers of Egypt, and for the bee that is in the land of Assyria" (7:18). The Lord will "shave with a razor that is hired in the parts beyond the River, even with the king of Assyria" (7:20; cf. 8:6-7a). These threats come from the period of the Syro-Ephraimitic war, but during the succeeding years Isaiah continued to proclaim Yahweh's purpose to use other nations, especially Assyria, to chastise His own people (9:11-12; 5:26-29; 10:5-6).

War, then, divinely instigated and divinely directed toward the disastrous defeat of His people, is Yahweh's chief method of punishing them.

The Assyrian, however, when seen close at hand, proves to be so arrogant and blasphemous that it is impossible to conceive of Yahweh's finding him a fit instrument to work His will (10:10-12, 15-18). Soon Yahweh will have finished punishing His own people, and will turn the full force of His wrath against His discarded tool, the Assyrian (10:24-25).

Since Yahweh thus completely controls the destinies of all nations, and directs the sword against the ones that have incurred His displeasure, nothing can befall His people contrary to His purpose.

Yahweh's power is available to His people, and is adequate for their protection against hostile armies. During the siege of Jerusalem by Syria and Israel, Isaiah is bidden to assure King Ahaz that the enemy kings are "two tails of smoking firebrands," and that nothing but faith in Yahweh is needed to withstand them (7:4, 7-9; cf. 8:12-13). We have seen that later, when Sennacherib is invading the land, Isaiah is equally certain that Yahweh purposes to crush the enemy (14:24-25; 17:12-14). Faith in Him will bring confidence and safety (28:16; 31:4-7; 30:15).

Sufficient answer to the solicitations of other nations to join them in rebellion against Assyria will be "that Jehovah hath founded Zion, and in her shall the afflicted of his people take refuge" (14:32). Egypt is utterly powerless to bring deliverance from Assyria (20:5-6; 30:1-3, 7). She herself is facing disaster (20:3-4; 18:4-6). "Woe unto them that go down to Egypt for help, and rely on horses, and trust in chariots because they are many, and in horsemen because they are very strong, but they look not unto the Holy One of Israel, neither seek Jehovah! . . . Now the Egyptians are men, and not God; and their horses flesh, and not spirit: and when Jehovah shall stretch out his hand, both he that helpeth shall stumble, and he that is helped shall fall, and they all shall be consumed together" (31:1, 3). "The Assyrian shall fall by the sword, not of man: and the sword, not of men, shall devour him" (31:8).

Isaiah is convinced, then, that war—either actual warfare, or preparedness by means of horses and chariots, fortresses, and offensive or defensive alliances—is not the right method. The only real power in history as in nature is Yahweh. In His hand the nations are but tools for His purposes. Quiet confidence, complete reliance upon Him in humility and faith is the method. But the method for what? The safety of Judah; its protection from enemies. Except in the pictures of the far-off ideal day, which are to be considered later, peace among nations is not contemplated. The question is, what will happen to Judah. If the nation conforms to Yahweh's will, cleanses its life from injustice and builds its national structure upon belief in His majestic power and righteous holiness, He will be a sure defense from its enemies. If it refuses to obey His will, He will chastise it with another nation which is likewise under His sway. And yet, if this other nation, a scourge in His hand, becomes arrogant and fails to realize His control, He will crush it and save Zion, His especial care, even without His people's wholly deserving it.

In short, the game is played not on the board where the nations move, but in the mind of Yahweh. His is the absolute power; He decrees the victor and achieves the victory. Not love, preeminently, but might, is the one potent influence. Only, the might is vested in no material display but in a spiritual force, which can subdue the undeserving and protect the favored ones.

In harmony with his conception of the uselessness and ungodliness of the machinery of war, when Isaiah's imagination leaps into the future to envisage conditions in some distant ideal day, he sees such things no longer needed.

It is Yahweh, not a mighty army, that will have brought the nation joyous prosperity and broken "the rod of his oppressor." "For all the armor of the armed man in the tumult, and the garments rolled in blood, shall be for burning, for fuel of fire. For unto us a child is born, unto us a son is given; and the government shall be upon his shoulder: and his name shall be called Wonderful, Counsellor, Mighty God, Everlasting Father, Prince of Peace" (9:3-6). Another picture of the divinely inspired, all-righteous Davidic king indicates that his word shall in some way have potency to quell all those who oppose his régime of justice. Isaiah could not consistently think of a warrior-king; he must be a completely conquering one, but it must be by spiritual means (11:1-5). The idea that peace shall result from the ideal king's righteous rule is stressed again in the third description (32:1, 16-18).

In this coming time of peace, when all fierceness and animosity, even among animals, shall be completely subdued, the perfect concord in Judah will be accompanied by a knowledge of Yahweh over all the earth, "as the waters cover the sea" (11:6-9). All nations will come to Zion for Yahweh's arbitration, "and he will judge between the nations, and will decide concerning many peoples; and they shall beat their swords into plowshares, and their spears into pruning-hooks; nation shall not lift up sword against nation, neither shall they learn war any more" (2:2-4).[5]

In the present, then, with unrighteousness rampant in all nations, with the nations hating one another and piling up armaments and plotting regardless of Yahweh's will, Yahweh has to exercise His control of history by decreeing victory for one or another of the fighting peoples. In the future day, however, when all men shall know Him and have regard for His ways, His righteousness dominant in national and international life

[5] This passage, which occurs also in Micah 4:1-3, may, of course, not be original in Isaiah.

shall bring lasting peace. The Yahweh of Isaiah, evidently, does not will war. While it exists, He directs it in line with His purposes, but real knowledge of Him and obedience to His purposes will do away with the causes of war.

We have followed the thought of the Hebrew writers as they have portrayed a God fighting with the help of His people "against the mighty," or urging His people to slaughter their rivals and assuring His aid; then, with Amos, a God protesting against the worst atrocities of warfare but not against the institution itself. We have something new in Isaiah's view of the futility and inherent evil of war, and hope of its being eventually superseded by purely spiritual means of achieving Yahweh's will. That war may not be an essential part of human experience, and that complete international understanding may be possible, seems to be suggested in the Old Testament first by Isaiah.

MICAH

Before the fall of Samaria, another prophet besides Isaiah raised his voice in Judah to denounce the sins of Yahweh's people. How long Micah worked is uncertain, but it is possible that his ministry extended into the reign of Manasseh, which seems to form the background of chapters 6:1 to 7:6.[6]

Micah thought of his prophetic office as "to declare unto Jacob his transgression, and to Israel his sin" (3:8). It is a question whether any of the hopeful passages come from him, and so it seems best to treat them separately in this discussion.

Micah is presenting Yahweh's dealings only with Israel and Judah, except by implication.

The Yahweh who is about to punish the greed and injustice and religious perversion of His people is both a God of right and a God of might. His only requirement of man is "to do justly, and to love kindness, and to walk humbly with thy God" (6:8). Neither the cult nor the holy city itself is of any vital concern to Him. The city, in fact, is the seat of corruption, and hence the chief object of Yahweh's destructive punishment. (Cf. 1:5; 3:10-12; 5:11; 6:9.) In His pleading in 6:3 we seem to catch a note of tenderness, but on the whole

[6] Cf. Bewer, *The Literature of the Old Testament*, pp. 118 f.

the people's sin, particularly that of the upper classes and the supposed religious leaders, permits only His unmitigated denunciation (2: 3; 3: 1-4; 6: 13-14, 16).

Yahweh's means of punishment are the forces of nature (1: 3-4), and other nations that He will bring against His doomed people (1: 8-16).

His relation to other nations is given only in this assumption of His being able to use them as His instruments, and in the reminiscence (6: 4-5) of His past deliverances and "righteous acts," which involves a reminder of His former protection of His people from their enemies.

It is clear that Micah's conception "never for a moment included the possibility of Yahweh's transferring His love to another nation,"[7] however completely He might crush His own.

The "hopeful passages," probably later additions to Micah's work by several different writers, offer the promise of the restoration of a remnant through Yahweh's power and favor (2: 12-13). This remnant, under Yahweh's immediate rule in Zion, will attain the summum bonum, "the former dominion" (4: 6-8). The conception of universal dominion is the climax of the announcement of the great ruler to come from Beth-lehem (5: 2, 4).

The lust for vengeance and conquest, with the assurance that Yahweh purposes this for His people, permeates the independent fragment in 5: 7-9, concluding with "Let thy hand be lifted up above thine adversaries, and let all thine enemies be cut off." Another passage exults in the conviction that Zion, baited by the assembled nations, will be enabled to turn upon them and brutally destroy them. This is Yahweh's purpose, and the spoil taken from them will be devoted to Him, "the Lord of the whole earth" (4: 11-13; cf. 5: 15). The song in 7: 7-13 breathes the same spirit of eager vindictiveness in its expression of confidence in Yahweh's ultimate exaltation of His own people and revenge upon the enemy. The closing prayer anticipates a time when Yahweh shall pardon all the iniquity of His people and resume toward them the "compassion" and "lovingkindness" promised

[7] Smith, J. M. P., *International Critical Commentary* on *Micah*, p. 25.

to the patriarchs (7:14-15, 18-20), but a concomitant of this lovingkindness to His own will be the utter confusion of the other nations and their cringing before "our God" (7:16-17).

Strikingly different is the conception in 4:1-3, a passage practically identical with Isaiah 2:2-4. Here the nations are to come to Zion of their own volition, to learn from Yahweh, and His arbitration among them will be so just and adequate that there will be no occasion for war any more.[8]

To summarize, we have in Micah's own work an all-powerful Yahweh, the God of this one people, but about to punish their unrighteousness with the utmost severity. The various additions deal, usually, with the hope of national restoration and triumph over enemies through Yahweh's power, followed by the worldwide recognition of His dominion. There is here, then, no advance in thought on this problem—not even the conservation of all of Isaiah's conceptions. Throughout the Old Testament, the evolution of ideas as to Yahweh's relation to war will be found to be a very halting process.

THE DEUTERONOMISTS

It was probably during the reign of Manasseh, when a reaction against the reforms of the preceding reign was carrying syncretism in religion to its furthest extreme and actually causing persecution of those in Judah who were most loyal to the religion of Yahweh, that certain devout Yahweh worshippers, of priestly-prophetic tendencies, undertook to interpret Yahweh's will for their own day through a revision and adaptation of the Hebrew laws. This new law code could not safely be made public during Manasseh's reign, but when Josiah was having the Temple repaired in 621 it was "found" by Hilkiah the priest and was made the basis of a great reformation, far-reaching in its influence upon Jewish thought and institutions.

The conception of God presented by the later Deuteronomists seems not essentially different from that in the original book, chapters 5-26 and 28, and so this discussion will include the

[8] An addition to this vision of future concord stresses the actual condition of henotheism. "For all the peoples walk every one in the name of his god; and we will walk in the name of Jehovah our God for ever and ever" (4:5).

entire present book, except the portions in its latter chapters which are assigned to E and P.

With its stress upon Yahweh's providence toward His people, Deuteronomy reiterates most frequently two of His gracious acts—His bringing them out of the land of Egypt, and His giving them the land of Canaan, as promised to their fathers.

Like E, Deuteronomy introduces the Decalogue with "I am Jehovah thy God, who brought thee out of the land of Egypt, out of the house of bondage" (5:6). The remembrance of this former bondage is often used as an incentive for obedience to Yahweh's law, particularly for the observance of the Sabbath day (5:15) and for generosity to a Hebrew bondservant released in the seventh year (15:12-15), while the signal manifestation of Yahweh's power and mercy in their deliverance must never be forgotten (6:20-22; 11:3-4; 13:5; 16:1-8, *passim;* 29:2).

Even more constantly, Deuteronomy recalls that Yahweh has given the Hebrews the land of Canaan to possess it, as He promised to Abraham, Isaac, and Jacob. They are urged—in accordance with the conceit that these reminiscences and exhortations and statutes were all uttered by Moses before the Israelites crossed the Jordan—to go in and take possession fearlessly (1:9, 20-21; 3:18; 4:1). They are admonished not to forget Yahweh when they have entered upon the enjoyment of all the good things labored for by others in that land (6:10-12). As a part of Yahweh's purpose for them, an evidence of His faithfulness and a stimulus to faithfulness on their part, the thought of their inheritance of the land recurs again and again (6:18, 23; 8:1; 10:11; 11:8-9, 21, 31; 12:10; 26:15).

Interestingly, although the "Amorites" and others in Canaan may be rightfully dispossessed according to Yahweh's plan, the nations which are rather closely related to the Hebrews—Edom, Moab, and Ammon—are thought of as having been established in their own territories by Yahweh and hence as not being open to attack and expulsion by the Hebrews (2:5, 9, 19, 21-22). Apparently, it is only their ancestral connection with the Hebrews that has caused Yahweh to exert himself for their welfare. The idea is not developed further, and falls far short of any conception of Yahweh's care for all nations, such as Amos presents.

In Yahweh's dealings with His own people, lovingkindness is predominant, blended with such a "jealousy" for their singlehearted devotion that disloyalty makes Him "angry" and necessitates punishment.

For faithless faintheartedness on the border of the promised land, "Jehovah heard the voice of your words, and was wroth, and sware, saying, Surely there shall not one of these men of this evil generation see the good land, which I sware to give unto your fathers, save Caleb . . ." (1:34-36). On account of the people's behavior He is wroth with Moses (1:37; 3:26; 4:21). "Jehovah thy God is a devouring fire, a jealous God" (4:24). However, the description of the future apostasy, punishment, and restoration shows a God who is fundamentally merciful (4:25-31).

Though these instances have been taken from the introductory chapters, the original book of Deuteronomy is also permeated with the conception of Yahweh's lovingkindness toward the faithful and jealous punishment of the wrongdoers. The reason for the prohibition of idolatry in the Decalogue is: "For I, Jehovah, thy God, am a jealous God, visiting the iniquity of the fathers upon the children, and upon the third and fourth generation of them that hate me; and showing lovingkindness unto thousands of them that love me and keep my commandments" (5:9-10; cf. 6:14-15; 7:9-10; 11:26-28; 13:17). The final chapter of the original work promises marvelous blessings for obedience (28:1-14), including: "Jehovah will cause thine enemies that rise up against thee to be smitten before thee . . . And thou shalt lend unto many nations, and thou shalt not borrow. And Jehovah will make thee the head, and not the tail; and thou shalt be above only, and thou shalt not be beneath" (28:7, 12b-13). Parallel to these blessings are the curses for disobedience (28:15-68), among which are pestilence, all kinds of incurable diseases, and defeat and captivity.

The idea that if Israel forgets Yahweh, and so incurs His anger, it will perish like the other nations, is found elsewhere (e.g., 7:4; 8:19a, 20a; 11:16-17; 29:22-28; 31:17). Moses gives the people a concrete example of Yahweh's great wrath when he relates how, after the incident of the golden calf, Yahweh said to him: "Let me alone, that I may destroy them, and blot out their name from under heaven; and I will make of thee a nation mightier and greater than they" (9:14). But his intercession for forty days saved Israel and Aaron from destruction by Yahweh (9:18-20).

Terrible as some of Yahweh's threats sound, Deuteronomy as a whole seems to contemplate disciplinary punishment rather than wrathful destruction. The spirit in which Yahweh inflicts punishments is explained: "And thou shalt consider in thy heart, that, as a man chasteneth his son, so Jehovah thy God chasteneth thee" (8:5).

Though not a part of the original book, the idea in chapter 30 that the outcome will be national repentance and restoration is in harmony with this conception of fatherly chastening (30: 1-3, 6-7). The relationship between Yahweh and His people is summed up in Moses' exhortation: "See, I have set before thee this day life and good, and death and evil; in that I command thee this day to love Jehovah thy God, to walk in his ways . . . I call heaven and earth to witness against you this day, that I have set before thee life and death, the blessing and the curse: therefore choose life, that thou mayest live, thou and thy seed; to love Jehovah thy God, to obey his voice, and to cleave unto him; for he is thy life, and the length of thy days; that thou mayest dwell in the land which Jehovah sware unto thy fathers, to Abraham, to Isaac, and to Jacob, to give them" (30:15-16a, 19-20).

Although the threats of punishment that we have already noted would indicate that fear is to be an important element in the motivation of obedience to Yahweh, the more unique characteristic of Deuteronomy is the emphasis seen here upon love to Yahweh. The familiar Shema, said by Jesus to be the greatest commandment, bids Israel: "Thou shalt love Jehovah thy God with all thy heart, and with all thy soul, and with all thy might" (6:5), and Yahweh's requirements are elsewhere summarized in similar vein. (Cf. 10:12-13; 11:1, 13, 22; 13:3*b*; 10:16; 30:6.)

Israel, thus beloved by Yahweh and supposed to respond with love to Him, is frequently contrasted with less favored nations. "For what great nation is there, that hath a god so nigh unto them, as Jehovah our God is whensoever we call upon him? And what great nation is there, that hath statutes and ordinances so righteous as all this law, which I set before you this day?" (4: 7-8) The sun and moon and stars have been allotted by Yahweh unto all the peoples under the whole heaven, "but Jehovah hath taken you, and brought you forth out of the iron furnace, out of Egypt, to be unto him a people of inheritance, as at this day" (4: 19-20; cf. 4: 33-35, 37-39). Yahweh's gracious love and faithfulness comprise the sole reason for His choice of Israel as a holy people (7: 6-8; 14: 2). The result of this choice will be unexampled health and prosperity for Israel (7: 14-15), and supremacy over other nations (15: 6; 26: 18-19; 28: 1-2).

Yahweh's choice of Israel must have been completely free, for He is all-sovereign, "God of gods, and Lord of lords, the great God, the mighty, and the terrible, who regardeth not persons, nor taketh reward" (10: 17). Though He is contrasted with other gods (3: 24), He is really the only significant deity in the universe. "Know therefore this day, and lay it to thy heart, that Jehovah he is God in heaven above and upon the earth beneath; there is none else" (4: 39; cf. 10: 14-15).

This one potent God is usually ready to fight for His people, but if in displeasure He withdraws His presence from their army, they cannot conquer (cf. 1: 42). None of the kingdoms in Canaan will escape Him.[9] The idea that Yahweh will destroy the enemies of His people, or the nations that obstruct their way, is frequently repeated (e.g., 6: 19; 7: 1-2, 16). There is no cause for Israel to fear any people, however great, since Yahweh's power and resourcefulness and favorable purpose can be trusted (7: 17-24; 1: 29-31), and great armies and military equipment are impotent against Him (20: 1-4).[10]

[9] Yahweh's attitude toward Sihon, king of the Amorites, is enlightening. He bids Israel contend with Sihon in battle, since He has given them his land (2: 24). In order to work Sihon's ruin, Yahweh hardens his heart and makes him refuse to grant Moses' diplomatic request for peaceful passage through his territory (2: 30-31), and finally Yahweh delivers him and all his people to the Israelites, who "utterly destroyed every inhabited city, with the women and the little ones" (2: 33-36).

Yahweh brings the same dreadful fate upon Og and his people, since they, too, are inhabiting territory that He purposes for the Israelites (3: 2-3).

[10] The Deuteronomic rules of warfare prescribe different methods of attack for the cities of the Canaanites from those to be used with distant cities. To the cities that are "very far off," an attacking Israelite army shall first "proclaim peace." If the city is peacefully opened, "all the people that are found therein shall become tributary unto thee, and shall serve thee"; if not, the Israelites shall lay siege, and when Yahweh gives them the city, they shall slay all the

However, the Israelites must not think that all these victories are the just desert of righteous conduct. On the contrary, they have been continually rebellious against Yahweh and have no claim to urge. Their military success is obtained for them by Yahweh for far different reasons—the wickedness of the nations in the land, and His faithfulness to His covenant with the Hebrew patriarchs (9:4-8, 22-24; 18:12).

After the land has been securely gained by Yahweh's help, old grievances are to be avenged: "Thou shalt blot out the remembrance of Amalek from under heaven; thou shalt not forget" (25:17-19).

In contrast to the treatment of foreigners en masse, the treatment prescribed by Deuteronomy for sojourners among the Israelites is, on the whole, remarkably considerate.

The sojourner is to be given his rights by the judges (1:16), and the Israelite is to love him, for two significant reasons—Yahweh loves the sojourner; and the Israelites were once themselves sojourners in the land of Egypt (10:18-19). The sojourner is classed with the Levite and the fatherless and the widow as a needy person, an object of kindness (14:29; 16:11; 24:17-22; 26:13).

A few distinctions are made, however, between Israelites and these foreign individuals among them. In the seventh year, brother Israelites are to be released from debt, but not foreigners (15:3). No foreigner may ever become king (17:15). No interest is to be taken on a loan made to an Israelite, but interest may be exacted from foreigners (23:19-20).

Between the sojourners, moreover, there are certain discriminations on the ground of nationality. Ammonites and Moabites are excluded from the assembly of Yahweh even to the tenth generation; "thou shalt not seek their peace nor their prosperity all thy days for ever" (23:3-6). An Edomite sojourner, on the other hand, since "he is thy brother," and an Egyptian, "because thou wast a sojourner in his land," may have the children of the third generation admitted to the assembly of Yahweh (23:7-8).

males, but save for themselves the women and children and all the spoil. "But of the cities of these peoples (in Canaan) that Jehovah thy God giveth thee for an inheritance, thou shalt save alive nothing that breatheth" (20:10-18).

The Israelites' camp must be kept scrupulously clean, to be fit for the presence of such a holy God as theirs (23:14).

The book of Deuteronomy contains in its Decalogue the pregnant words: "Thou shalt not kill" (5:17). We have need to ask what their limitations are here.

Already we have had frequent occasion to note one important exception: enemies in war not only may, but must, be killed, according to Yahweh's own command, and it is through Yahweh's own action that the nations in Canaan are wiped out.

Blood revenge is another exception. The "lex talionis" prescribes: "Thine eye shall not pity; life shall go for life, eye for eye, tooth for tooth, hand for hand, foot for foot" (19:21). To prevent the shedding of "innocent blood," cities of refuge are provided for the "manslayer," who kills accidentally (4:41-42; 19:2-3), but the willful murderer is to be delivered by the elders of the city into the hand of the avenger of blood, to be killed (19:12). The basic ground of distinction between the manslayer and the murderer is whether he hated the victim, and so planned to kill him (19:11).

Besides the murderer, several other criminals are to be put to death.[11] Only the guilty individual is to be killed: "The fathers shall not be put to death for the children, neither shall the children be put to death for the fathers; every man shall be put to death for his own sin" (24:16).

"Thou shalt not kill," then, applies to fellow-Israelites and sojourners, who are not guilty of any crime requiring the death penalty.

To summarize our findings with regard to the Yahweh portrayed in Deuteronomy, He is a God abiding in heaven, supreme over all nations and all other gods, who in His grace has chosen one nation to love and to cherish. Incidental to this love for His chosen nation is His destruction of the others who may stand in its way or imperil its loyalty to Him.

Yahweh's grace toward His people prompts not only their protection and their establishment in the land purposed for them,

[11] The false prophet that tries to lead people to worship other gods, or any prophet who presumptuously speaks in Yahweh's name something not actually commanded by Him (13:5; 18:20); an apostate relative (13:8-10); the inhabitants of a city which is disloyal to Yahweh (13:15-18); any man or woman that worships other gods (17:5); a rebellious son (21:21); those who have violated the laws of chastity (22:13-27); and one who steals and enslaves an Israelite (24:7).

but also, and supremely, the revelation of His will through ordinances designed to make channels for that outflowing of love and grateful obedience with which His people ought to respond to Him.

All about them are the seductive influences of the base religious observances of other peoples, supposedly pleasing to their gods. In the midst is this holy people, chosen out of all the rest to love Him and serve Him. In the soil of their national remembrance, the brotherly conduct and the purified worship pleasing to Him should strike deep root. Obedient service will bring life and joy and prosperity; disobedience is the way of death. Yahweh's love is not incompatible here with anger, and His mercy is only for those who respond to His overtures and are faithful to Him.

When unfaithfulness may necessitate fearful chastisement, He can use other nations to punish His own people, but there is never any hint of His transferring His favor to some other people, and giving them the chance to serve Him and experience His grace. With all His love and mercy and universal sovereignty, He is Israel's God, and Israel alone is or can be His people.

Zephaniah

The wild hordes of the Scythians, spreading terror and destruction as they swept through western Asia, were descending upon Syria in 626 B.C. Believing that Judah would fall a prey to their invasion, both Zephaniah and Jeremiah were roused to prophetic activity—to the effort to show their people how Yahweh was about to manifest Himself. The fact that the Scythians actually did leave Judah untouched does not take from Zephaniah's interpretation of Yahweh's activity its significance for our study.

Zephaniah sees in the oncoming Scythians the agent that Yahweh will use to bring in His great "day" of judgment. Yahweh has "prepared a sacrifice" and "consecrated his guests" for the slaughter (1:7). He will "consume all things from off the face of the ground" (1:2). In His awful day of trouble and desolation and darkness, no man will be able to stand before His wrath (1:14-18).

The prophet is especially concerned to warn his own people of Judah, in order that, "before the fierce anger of Jehovah come upon you," the "meek of the earth, that have kept His ordinances" may with renewed zeal seek righteousness, since then it may be that they will be hid in the day of Yahweh's anger (1:3). Judah's sin is the cause of her coming disaster (3: 5, 7).

Not only Yahweh's own people, but many other nations, including Philistia (2:4-5), Ethiopia and Assyria (2:12-13), will be destroyed in the day of His wrath.[12]

A passage which is perhaps an addition to Zephaniah's work[13] holds out the promise that in the day when Yahweh rises to assemble the kingdoms and pour upon them His fierce anger, He will purify Judah of all the proud and wicked, and "will leave in the midst of thee an afflicted and poor people, and they shall take refuge in the name of Jehovah"; this remnant will live in perfect righteousness and security (3:8, 11-13). Inserted in this oracle is another implying that from the other nations, too, a devout remnant will be saved, who will all eventually worship Yahweh (3:9-10).

The final appendix to the book (3:14-20) is an exultant song of national joy, celebrating the restoration and exaltation of Jerusalem under Yahweh as King, and the overthrow of all her enemies.

The Yahweh of Zephaniah's own prophecies thus appears as a God of righteousness who is about to visit both Judah and the other nations with terrible destruction in fierce anger.

Some of the additions strike a nationalistic note not present in the original; others stress the universalistic idea, and look be-

[12] A later insertion, 2:8-10, makes Moab and Ammon the target of "Jehovah of hosts, the God of Israel" for reviling His people. The motive of retaliation in this threat is in contrast to the restraint of the oracles against the other nations, which do not specify their sins, but create the cumulative impression of a clean sweep of doom over all the nations.
A still later addition, 2:11 (cf. Smith, J. M. P., *International Critical Commentary* on *Micah, Zephaniah,* and *Nahum,* pp. 228 f.), quite inconsistently with the rest of this chapter represents the nations as worshipping Yahweh after the terrible exhibition of His power.
[13] Cf. Smith, J. M. P., *op. cit.,* pp. 246-252.

yond the coming catastrophe to a time when Yahweh shall be worshipped by all peoples.

Nahum

The mighty empire that had captured and swallowed up the northern kingdom, that had held the southern kingdom and all the neighboring peoples as vassals for over a century and had successfully crushed the repeated efforts of an ever-insurgent nationalism to throw off foreign domination—this empire was now tottering, and the lesser nations were watching its struggle with an all-consuming eagerness for the destruction of their brutal conqueror. Fear was giving way to exultation as the capture of Nineveh by the Medes and Babylonians seemed ever more certain. Many in Judah saw in this event the hand of Yahweh, and the poet Nahum voiced this conviction in a song of triumphant hatred.

Nahum's remarkably vivid descriptions of the confusion and terror of the attack upon Nineveh gain their significance for our study from the fact that all this is the result of Yahweh's purpose. It is in reality Yahweh who is slaughtering this lion who has made prey of the smaller nations (2: 13a).

Interpolations stress Yahweh's purpose to bring relief to His own people through this destruction of their enemy (1: 13, 15c; 2: 2a).

The acrostic prefixed to Nahum's poem presents a conception of Yahweh's character that is consistent with Nahum's view. "Jehovah is a jealous God and avengeth; . . . Jehovah taketh vengeance on his adversaries, and he reserveth wrath for his enemies" (1: 2; cf. 1: 8-9). All nature cowers before the might of this God, and "who can abide the fierceness of his anger? his wrath is poured out like fire" (1: 3b-6). Toward His own, Yahweh presents a very different aspect: "Jehovah is good, a stronghold in the day of trouble; and he knoweth them that take refuge in him" (1: 7).

According to Nahum, then, through battle Yahweh is wrathfully requiting the enemy of His people for cruel oppression of them and of others. He cares preëminently for Israel, but all the nations that have suffered will join in exultation over the death-blow which He is dealing to their foe (3:19).

HABAKKUK

The prophetic work of Habakkuk probably began during the reign of Jehoiakim, about 605, and continued for some time after the first capture of Jerusalem by the Babylonians in 597, perhaps until about 590. He witnessed "violence" and "iniquity" and "perverted justice" within the nation—followed by the onslaught of a conquering nation even more presumptuous and impious than Judah. Why did Yahweh not interfere?

As portrayed by Habakkuk, Yahweh is a God always about to act in forceful vindication of His moral government of the world.

He answers the plea for justice within the nation by raising up the Chaldeans (1:5-9). When, however, this godless, self-confident army proves an instrument ill suited to the establishment of righteousness, it must be that Yahweh is about to visit punishment upon it (1:12b; 2:7-8a, 16b-17).

The prophet is reassured as to Yahweh's purpose to overthrow the iniquitous Chaldeans by an impressive vision accorded him in answer to his pleading for Yahweh to revive His work and "in wrath remember mercy" (3:2)—a vision of Yahweh coming in glory and power as a mighty warrior, armed with all the forces of physical nature to fight for the deliverance of His people (3: 5-13). Meanwhile, until the fulfillment of the vision, "the righteous shall live by his faith" (2:4b).

An addition to the psalm that portrays this advent of Yahweh protests that, whatever misfortunes may come,

I will joy in the God of my salvation.
Jehovah, the Lord, is my strength. (3:18b-19a)

Two interpolations in chapter 2 carry us out beyond the horizon of Habakkuk's thought of Yahweh's omnipotence to the conception of all the earth as responding to Yahweh (2:14, 20).

Habakkuk, then, presents a God of righteousness who has as yet done nothing in the present generation to manifest His righteousness according to the orthodox ideas of retributive justice. The eye of faith, however, glimpses His invincible might and His purpose to wield it soon for the destruction of the wicked and the salvation of His people.

JEREMIAH

Aroused to activity, like Zephaniah, by the Scythian invasion of Palestine in 626, Jeremiah continued his prophetic work for at least forty years, until after the fall of Jerusalem in 586. Though naturally sensitive, and shrinking from his tremendous commission from Yahweh, when once embarked upon his prophetic task Jeremiah fearlessly faced his generation with Yahweh's severe message. Reinterpreting the "foe from the north" as the Chaldeans, Jeremiah clung to his conviction of Yahweh's purpose to use such an instrument, with a consistency lacking in Isaiah's work. "Despised and rejected of men," subjected to physical suffering and spiritual anguish, the prophet Jeremiah was thrown back upon Yahweh as his one source of courage and strength, with an intimacy of personal communion that marked a step forward in the Hebrew experience of God.

It is fruitless to try to harmonize perfectly the attitudes attributed to Yahweh in Jeremiah's utterances. As in Hosea's case, Jeremiah finds Yahweh baffled by His people's almost unbelievable unfaithfulness and unresponsiveness, longing and pleading and threatening and struggling—and absolute consistency of expression is not to be expected. We can only endeavor to distinguish the different attitudes that he does express, and perhaps find which ones are dominant. As in Hosea's portrayal, there may be a fundamentally consistent divine purpose, which is sometimes almost obscured by the difficulty of finding an adequate method for its achievement.

Yahweh, according to Jeremiah, has a definite and significant relation to other nations besides Israel. In the very beginning, Jeremiah is appointed "a prophet unto the nations" (1:5b), set over them "to pluck up and to break down and to destroy and to overthrow, to build and to plant" (1: 9b-10). In accordance with this commission, he voices Yahweh's threat of punishment against Egypt, Judah, Edom, Ammon, and Moab, "for all the nations are uncircumcised, and all the house of Israel are uncircumcised in heart" (9: 25-26). Later, the prophet has to cause all the nations,[14] including Judah, to drink the cup of the wine of Yahweh's wrath, to be experienced through the sword which He will send among them (25: 15-26a). (Cf. 25: 29; 27: 2-15; 28: 14.)

The thought of Yahweh's punishment of other nations is elaborated impressively in the oracles against Egypt, Philistia, Moab, Ammon, Edom, and Elam, in chapters 46 to 49.[15] In the main, these prophecies do not seem vindictive, though Ammon is to be conquered in retaliation for the conquest of part of Israel's territory (49: 1-2). The general impression is, rather, that Yahweh is about to use Nebuchadnezzar to make a clean sweep of punishment of these nations for arrogant self-confidence and general wickedness, "magnifying themselves toward Him." The fierceness and the vivid imagery of these oracles may be illustrated by such passages as the following: "Egypt riseth up like the Nile . . . Go up, ye horses; and rage, ye chariots; and let the mighty men go forth . . . For that day is a day of the Lord, Jehovah of hosts, a day of vengeance, that he may avenge him of his adversaries: and the sword shall devour and be satiate, and shall drink its fill of their blood; for the Lord, Jehovah of hosts, hath a sacrifice in the north country by the river Euphrates" (46: 8a, 9a, 10). "O thou sword of Jehovah, how long will it be ere thou be quiet? put up thyself into thy scabbard; rest, and be still. How canst thou be quiet, seeing Jehovah hath given thee a charge? Against Ashkelon, and against the seashore, there hath he appointed it" (47: 6-7). "Cursed be he that doeth the work of Jehovah negligently; and cursed be he that keepeth his sword from blood" (48: 10). When Nebuchadnezzar's army devastates these nations, it will

[14] Jeremiah's original prophecy probably did not actually deal with "all the kingdoms of the world"; a later editor has added Sheshach, or Babylon. This idea of the universality of the slaughter at the hand of Yahweh is well expressed in 25: 32-33.

[15] These oracles may have come from Jeremiah himself, but probably the others in the collection are from a later hand (cf. Bewer, op. cit., pp. 155, 161, 163). We doubtless owe to an editor, also, the idea of restoration added to the prophecies against Ammon (49: 6) and Elam (49: 39).

signify that Yahweh, whose instrument he is, is fighting victoriously against the gods of the vanquished nations (43: 12-13; 46: 25; 48: 7, 13).[16]

The mighty God who can thus punish all nations, including Judah, and who is also in control of nature (5: 22-24; 14: 22), "the living God" (23: 36c), filling heaven and earth (23: 24), is nevertheless "Jehovah of hosts, the God of Israel" (e.g., 7: 3; 16: 9; 19: 3, 15; et al.). The "prophet unto the nations" is still preëminently a prophet to the people of Judah, for it is their relation with Yahweh that is of supreme importance.

The nation that Yahweh loves has grievously sinned. His people have defiled His land (2: 7; 3: 9; 16: 18), worshipping other gods (2: 28; 3: 6; 5: 19b; 7: 18). Yahweh wants loyal devotion—expressed, however, not through the cult but through obedience to His requirements of justice and righteousness (7: 5-6; 22: 3, 13-14). The conduct of Yahweh's people is entirely unnatural. No other nation has changed its gods, even though they be "no gods" (2: 10-11). The birds of the heavens observe their appointed times, according to the laws of their nature, but Yahweh's people do not so observe His law (8: 7). When men fall, they usually rise again, but Jerusalem's backsliding is perpetual (8: 4-5; cf. 2: 32; 18: 13-15). These people are so caught in the grip of evil habits that evil has become a second nature to them: "Can the Ethiopian change his skin, or the leopard his spots? then may ye also do good, that are accustomed to do evil" (13: 23).

Such conduct arouses the burning wrath of Yahweh. "I myself will fight against you with an outstretched hand and with a strong arm, even in anger, and in wrath, and in great indignation" (21: 5). The frequency with which this attitude is ascribed to Yahweh shows how fundamental a part of Jeremiah's conception it must have been. (Cf. 4: 4, 8; 7: 20, 29b; 10: 24-25; 11: 17b; 12: 13c; 15: 14c; 17: 4c; 18: 20b, 23d; 21:

[16] It seems quite certain that Jeremiah held consistently to the view that Yahweh would use the Babylonian army as His tool, and the passages predicting the fall of Babylon (25: 12-14, chs. 50-51) should not be attributed to him. They should be placed, rather, in the last years of the Babylonian exile (cf. Bewer, *op. cit.*, p. 213). The conception is that Yahweh will bring a company of great nations to destroy Babylon (50: 9-10); Israel and Judah will have their wrongs fully avenged: "As Babylon hath caused the slain of Israel to fall, so at Babylon shall fall the slain of all the land" (51: 49), and themselves will escape the disaster in Babylonia by returning to their own land (51: 45).

Pre-Exilic Prophets

12*b*; 23:19-20; 25:7, 15, 37-38; 32:30-32; 33:5; 42:18; 44:3, 6, 8.) The prophet cannot refrain from utterance, because he is "full of the wrath of Jehovah" (6:11*a*). Yahweh's soul must "be avenged on such a nation as this" (5:9, 29; 9:9).

In other passages, Yahweh's sternness and severity are stressed, without mention of anger. In the time of their trouble, His people will cry to Him to save them, but He will not listen; let the other gods whom they have worshipped try to save them (2:27-28; 11:11; 14:12; 16:13). Yahweh has now cast off His "dearly beloved" (12:7-8), taken away from this people His lovingkindness and tender mercies (16:5*b*). The strongest soap cannot wash away their iniquity (2:22). Only false prophets cry "peace" when the situation calls for punishment (6:14; 8:11; 23:17). (Cf. 4:28; 13:14, 27*b*; 15:6; 16:18; 23:29, 39-40.)

Intercession is useless now, conditions are too hopeless (7:16; 11:14; 14:11). Even Moses and Samuel would not be able to prevail upon Yahweh to relent (15:1).

The terrible punishment that Yahweh will visit upon Judah is constantly reiterated. Sometimes the threat is picturesquely suggestive—a lion, wolf, or leopard (4:7; 5:6), or serpents that cannot be charmed (8:17), or wormwood and gall (9:15; 23:15); sometimes it is a vaguely menacing destruction, to be consumed (8:13) or gleaned (6:9) or melted (9:7) or broken like a potter's vessel (19:11). Elsewhere, the methods of punishment are specified, usually the sword, famine, and pestilence (14:12*b*; 21:7; 24:10; 29:17-18; 34:17; 38:2; 42:16-17, 22). Sometimes, an awful enemy from the north, or from a far country, is threatened, referring at first to the Scythians (1:15; 4:16-18; 5:15-16), and in still other passages the king of Babylon is definitely named as the instrument of Yahweh's purpose against His people (20:4*c*-5; 21:10; 32:2-3). To be scattered, and to serve their enemies in an unknown land, is the climax of many of the oracles of doom (13:24; 15:14; 17:4; 18:17).

Over against these passages of unrelieved doom, we have many others which present Yahweh in a quite different aspect. He earnestly pleads with His people to show Him why they have so deserted Him (2:5, 31, 36). "Thus saith Jehovah, Stand ye in the old ways and see, and ask for the old paths, where is the good way; and walk therein, and ye shall find rest for your souls" (6:16). Through all the prophets He has besought them to return to Him (25:5) and He still cherishes a hope that they will respond (6:8).

If they will return to Him in penitence and with the determination to amend their ways, He is ready and eager to accept and restore them. "Return, ye backsliding children, I will heal your backslidings" (3:22a; cf. 3:12-14; 4:1-2; 5:1; 7:3-7; 18:7-8; 26:3, 13; 35:15).

Yahweh is the one adequate help of His people, the "hope of Israel, the Saviour thereof in time of trouble" (14:8; 3:22b-23; 9:23-24), the "fountain of living waters" (2:13; 17:13).

Occasionally, His attitude toward them assumes a depth of tenderness hardly equaled in the words of any other prophet except Hosea. He longs to have them call Him, "my Father," and cleave to Him (3:4-5a, 19; 13:11). In Jeremiah's expression of his hope for the restoration of the lost northern tribes, he gives the most appealing portrayal of Yahweh's love. "Yea, I have loved thee with an everlasting love: therefore with lovingkindness have I drawn thee" (31:3). Rachel need weep no longer; her children will come again from the land of the enemy. Ephraim, after having been chastised, is repentant, and Yahweh's love will restore him. "Is Ephraim my dear son? is he a darling child? for as often as I speak against him, I do earnestly remember him still: therefore my heart yearneth for him; I will surely have mercy upon him, saith Jehovah" (31:20).

In keeping with the conception of Yahweh's love and desire to save, Jeremiah thinks of Him as promising for the days to come: "I will put my law in their inward parts, and in their heart will I write it; and I will be their God, and they shall be my people. And they shall teach no more every man his neighbor, and every man his brother, saying, Know Jehovah; for they shall all know me, from the least of them unto the greatest of them, saith Jehovah: for I will forgive their iniquity, and their sin will I remember no more" (31:33-34).[17]

---

[17] The other type of prophecy of restoration, according to which a remnant of Yahweh's flock will be gathered from all the countries, brought back to the fold, and blessed with every kind of prosperity, with a righteous Davidic king called "Yahweh our righteousness" reigning wisely and justly over Judah and Israel (23:3-8; 33:14-18), probably comes from the late exilic or the postexilic period (cf. Bewer, *op. cit.*, p. 408). Similar passages, promising

The man whom Yahweh has chosen to bear His message and almost to incarnate His idea must live a lonely life, misunderstood and hated, accused of treason though giving his life for his people, frequently tortured in body and mind. Although he is thus in a significant sense a "suffering servant" of Yahweh, the prophet reflects in his attitude toward his own enemies the angry, punitive aspect rather than the forgiving love of the divine character. Persecuted almost beyond endurance, Jeremiah commits his cause to Yahweh, confident that He will bring vengeance upon his enemies (11:20-23; 15:15; 18:19-23; 20:4, 11-12). "Pull them out like sheep for the slaughter" (12:3). "Bring upon them the day of evil, and destroy them with double destruction" (17:18). Yahweh had promised to strengthen and deliver him (1:8, 19; 15:20-21), and it must be that He would do it through the destruction of his persecutors. The death of Hananiah (28:16-17) and the dire fate foretold for Pashhur (20:6), Shemaiah (29:24-32), and Jehoiakim (36:30-31) seem to show that Yahweh is thus fulfilling His promise.

To summarize, the Yahweh of Jeremiah is definitely "the God of Israel." Though He is complete sovereign of the world, His care and tenderness go out to just one people. The mighty Yahweh is in control of everything except the stubborn human heart—He is baffled by the unnatural ingratitude and callous faithlessness of His disobedient people. Though He yearns over them, His wrath must burn at such conduct, and He must visit their iniquity with dreadful punishments. Always, however, the way lies open for repentant return to Him and consequent healing from Him—and beyond the chastisement the divine love sees a restored people, to whom He Himself will give a "new heart" to know and obey Him.

deliverance from captivity and punishment of those who have oppressed Israel and Judah, comprise chapter 30 and are scattered through other parts of the book.

CHAPTER V

WRITINGS FROM THE EXILIC PERIOD

1. Ezekiel—2. Holiness Code—3. Lamentations—4. Other Fragments of Poetry and Prophecy—5. Historical Writings with the Point of View of Deuteronomy—6. Deutero-Isaiah

EZEKIEL

Ezekiel the priest, carried into Babylon with the deportation of the élite of Judah in 597 B.C., performed his prophetic ministry against a background of national chaos and collapse. To a people who had failed to take warning from the first capture of Jerusalem by the Babylonians, Ezekiel cried, from exile, that their more complete doom was inevitable if they persisted in their profanation of Yahweh's holiness, and he drove home his message with grotesquely impressive object lessons. Meanwhile he felt an almost overwhelming spiritual responsibility toward his companions in captivity, and became for them the source of constant admonition and of illumination as to Yahweh's requirements and purposes.

With the fall of Jerusalem in 586, Ezekiel's proclamation of destruction was fulfilled. As Yahweh's spokesman, he must now deal with a people politically crushed, carried away from their own land, living for the most part in scattered communities amid the seductive culture of their Babylonian conquerors, and uncertain as to how to interpret their calamity. Had Yahweh been defeated by the gods of the Babylonians, or had He deserted His people in their hour of desperate need? Some reconciliation of their national ignominy with the conception of a God who both cared for them and had the power to help them was needed if that God were to remain a reality to them; some hopeful assurance of national restoration must come if national morale were to be revived. Their uniqueness in religion and their national identity were both at stake. To Ezekiel

—and to many unknown sharers in his conviction that Yahweh, having punished, would eventually reclaim His people—is due that stimulation of national hope and religious idealism which saved this people from assimilation by the surrounding civilization, redirected their thinking toward the possibility of avoiding in the future the disastrous violations of Yahweh's requirements, and produced a group ardent enough to brave the dangers of return to their land, when that was permitted by their new Persian sovereign.

Ezekiel conceives of Yahweh's relations with other nations only as a by-product of His relations with Israel. On the stage of history there are two main actors—Yahweh and His people Israel; other nations are now the background against which Israel's acting stands out the more impressively, now the audience witnessing and applauding Yahweh's dealings with Israel, now called in as supernumeraries to be marshaled by Yahweh against Israel, now wrathfully attacked by Yahweh for injuries against Israel, and driven from the stage in utter confusion.

The nations serve as background when Yahweh tells Ezekiel that "many peoples of a strange speech and of a hard language" would hearken to his prophetic message more responsively than stiff-hearted Israel (3:5-7); when Yahweh asserts that Jerusalem has done wickedness "more than the nations" (5:5-7); and when He shows that her sins and abominations are worse than those of her sisters, Samaria and Sodom (16:46-52).

The nations as audience are to witness Israel's punishment (5:8, 14-15) and her profanation (22:16) and to mock Israel (22:4b-5), though later they are to be punished in Yahweh's "jealousy" and "wrath" for thus heaping shame upon Israel (36:6b-7). Similarly, when Yahweh punishes Tyre (27:35-36; 28:19) and Egypt (32:10) others look on, though now in trembling amazement.

When called in as Yahweh's instrument of chastisement, a nation's individuality is often swallowed up in its identification with Yahweh's purpose, so that it is now His sword, and now the sword of the king of Babylon, which shall be wielded against Israel (ch. 21, *passim;* cf. 12:13; 17:20) or against Tyre (32:10-12a). In other cases, the foreigners are "strangers," or "the worst of the nations," into whose power Yahweh gives the people whom He is castigating (7:21, 24a; 11:9; cf. 23:9, 22-24, 28-29; 26:7-14; 28:7; 29:17-20; 30:10-11, 24-25).

As we have already discovered, the Yahweh of Ezekiel concerns Himself with the chastisement of other nations besides Israel. This, however, does not indicate a divine interest in those nations per se. In every case, the nation that He is to punish has in some way impiously thrust itself upon the scene where He is dealing with His own people, and so, in retaliation, must be chased off the stage. The most usual offense is to have jeered at Judah in the day of her discomfiture by the Babylonians. (Cf. chs. 25-29; 35:5-6, 10-11, 15.) When in Yahweh's vengeance Ammon, Moab, Edom, Philistia, Tyre, Sidon, and Egypt have all been duly requited, "there shall be no more a pricking brier unto the house of Israel, nor a hurting thorn of any that are round about them, that did despite unto them" (28:24).

Yahweh is concerned to have other nations besides Israel realize His power and holiness, "know that I am Yahweh." This seems to involve no significant relationship with Him such as is open to Israel. Rather, a sort of divine pride requires that the sanctity of His name be vindicated in the sight of all nations. His dealings with Israel, then, are partially motivated by a kind of dread lest His ability to protect and exalt His own people be called in question by others.

Turning to the problem of Yahweh's attitude toward His own people and His methods of dealing with them, we notice first that He aims to be perfectly fair to Israel, and gives due warning of the punishment that is to be visited upon her sins, by sending a prophet to this rebellious people, "whether they will hear, or whether they will forbear" (2:3-7; 3:4-11, 27). He makes Ezekiel a "watchman," to give warning to the wicked individuals (3:17-21; 33:7-9). The various object lessons divinely suggested to the prophet are intended for "signs" to the house of Israel (e.g., 4:3b; 12:6c). "It may be they will consider, though they are a rebellious house" (12:3c).

The hint of the possibility of averting national calamity through national reformation is nowhere emphatically developed —the people in general seem too corrupt to permit cherishing such a hope. With regard to individuals, however, the case is quite different. Though the people as a whole could not be saved by the presence among them of the most righteous individuals conceivable, even Noah, Daniel, and Job (14:14, 16, 18, 20), still, righteous individuals will save themselves, and the chance to become righteous by turning "from all his sins which he hath committed" and keeping Yahweh's statutes, is at any time open to a man. (Cf. 18:21-22; 33:14-16.) "The soul that sinneth, it shall die" (18:4, 20)—that soul, though no other—but Yahweh would fain have the wicked reform his ways and live (18:23, 30-32; 33:11).

The sins for which a soul must die are several times enumerated. Yahweh's requirements are both cultic and ethical, apparently on the same plane (18:5-9; 22:6-12; 33:25-26). The sins for which the nation as a social group is being constantly arraigned likewise fall into both classes, but cultic sins predominate—particularly the abominations of idolatry (e.g., 6:4-7; 14:7-8; 16:17; 20:28, 32, 39; 22:3-4a), defiling Yahweh's sanctuary (5:11a; 8:5-18), and other profanations of His holiness such as breaking His sabbaths (20:13, 16, 21). Israel's unfaithfulness is the more execrable in view of the kindness that Yahweh has heaped upon her in the past (16:6-14), choosing her, whose parents were the Amorite and the Hittite (16:3, 45), as the object of His very special favor.

Yahweh's attitude in punishing His people is wrathful in the extreme. "So will I gather you in mine anger and in my wrath, and I will lay you there, and melt you" (22:20b; cf. 5:13; 6:12; 7:3, 8, 12, 14, 19; 13:13, 15a; 16:38, 42; 20:33; 22:31).

He is decidedly resourceful as to methods of chastisement. His means of destruction include famine, usually accompanied by pestilence (4:16-17; 5:12, 16-17; 6:11-12; 7:15; 14:13, 19, 21), stoning (16:40; 23:47); fire (15:6-8; 16:41; 23:47), and evil beasts (5:17; 14:15, 21). His most efficacious instrument, however, is the sword. "Thus saith Jehovah, Say, A sword, a sword, it is sharpened, and also furbished; it is sharpened that it may make a slaughter; . . . Cry and wail, son of man, for it is upon my people, . . . I have set the threatening sword against all their gates, that their heart may melt, and their stumblings be multiplied: ah! it is made a lightning, it is pointed for slaughter" (21:9-10a, 12a, 15; cf. 5:12, 17; 6:3, 7, 11-12; 7:15; 11:8, 10; 12:14; 14:17, 21; 16:40; 17:21; 21:3-5;

23:47; 24:21; 33:2). The climax of the punishment is, of course, for the chosen people to be "scattered among the nations" (5:10*b*, 12; 11:16; 12:11, 14-15; 17:21; 22:15; 36: 16-19).

However, once Yahweh has defended His outraged holiness by thus punishing Israel, He must consider how to convince the other nations that He Himself has brought this calamity upon His people and that He is able to do with the nations whatever He wills to do. The presence of Israel, apparently helpless, in exile, profanes Yahweh's "holiness" by giving the nations a chance to think slightingly of His power. He must restore His people, not out of compassion for them, but to recover His own prestige (36:22-24, 32, 36). A chastened remnant will be salvaged, to become a people truly belonging to Yahweh (6:8-9*a*). "And I will give them one heart, and I will put a new spirit within you; and I will take the stony heart out of their flesh, and will give them a heart of flesh; that they may walk in my statutes, and keep mine ordinances, and do them: and they shall be my people, and I will be their God" (11:19-20; cf. 12:16; 14:11; 16:60-63; 20:41; 36:24-31). "And I will set up one shepherd over them, and he shall feed them, even my servant David; he shall feed them, and he shall be their shepherd" (34:23; cf. 34:24-26, 30-31; 37:21-24).

Thus, through the restoration of a chastened and purified Israel, and through the punishment of the nations that have dared to exult over her misfortunes, Yahweh will give the nations a two-fold manifestation of His power to protect the sanctity of His name.

To summarize, the Yahweh of Ezekiel desires primarily that His divine adequacy and His requirements of cultic and ethical holiness shall be felt by His people and witnessed by the other nations. To this end, He uses His destructive might to punish the profanation of His name by Israel, and afterwards turns upon the other nations and reclaims and exalts Israel. All nations must recognize Him; Israel alone can be His people and have Him for her God. Here we have a God of universal power without universal care.

HOLINESS CODE

One of the unnamed religious leaders who worked during the Exile to maintain the morale and the idealism of the people of Yahweh was the author of the so-called "Holiness Code," Leviticus 17-26. This writer's work shows many similarities to that of Ezekiel, and clearly comes from the same school of thought. We should probably place his writing shortly after Ezekiel's work, which closed about 570 B.C.[1]

In the Holiness Code, Yahweh has dealings with other nations only as He drives them out of the land which His people are to inherit or as He threatens to punish His people's disobedience by war and conquest and captivity, or as citizens of other nations become "sojourners" among Yahweh's own people. Yahweh seems to be in control of all nations, but His ordinances are for only one, and this one alone has been chosen to manifest His holiness.

It is noteworthy, however, that the expulsion of the former inhabitants of Canaan is here justified, as it were, by the abominations which they had committed, particularly their sexual impurities, and that Yahweh's people are threatened with a like punishment for a like defilement. There is thus a trace of impartiality in punishment, but that impression rather fades beneath the consideration that Yahweh had never taught any of these other nations how to observe His holiness, and hence their defilement was, from this point of view, inevitable. Impartiality would require equal opportunity to avoid guilt, as well as like punishment for the same sin—and the opportunity to know Yahweh and so avoid profaning His holiness is here given to only one nation, with no commission to share it with other nations. (Cf. Lev. 18: 3-4, 24-29; 20: 22-24.)

Obedience to Yahweh's law by His people will be rewarded with rich crops and peaceful security and signal victory over enemies (Lev. 26: 3-13). On the other hand, Yahweh will fearfully punish disobedience, using pestilence and famine and enemy nations as the instruments of His chastisement (Lev. 26: 16-39).

---

[1] Cf. Bewer, *The Literature of the Old Testament*, pp. 183 f.

Within the nation, relations between members of the community are based on the highest possible principle, which needs only the broader interpretation of Jesus to make it pregnant of international good-will. In this code, however, its reference is only to fellow-members of Yahweh's chosen group. "Thou shalt not hate thy brother in thy heart: thou shalt surely rebuke thy neighbor, and not bear sin because of him. Thou shalt not take vengeance, nor bear any grudge against the children of thy people; but thou shalt love thy neighbor as thyself: I am Jehovah'' (Lev. 19: 17-18).

Sojourners are to be treated as members of the Hebrew community—not wronged, but loved "as thyself" (Lev. 19: 33-34; 24: 22). All the people, indeed, are but sojourners on land which really belongs to Yahweh (Lev. 25: 23).

One important distinction is made between sojourners and Israelites. Children of sojourners may be bought as slaves and kept in perpetual servitude, like members of neighboring nations, but fellow-Israelites must not be reduced to actual slavery, and must be released entirely in the year of jubilee—for the interesting reason that Israelites are all Yahweh's bondmen, and so must not be slaves to one another (Lev. 25: 39-46). On similar grounds, an Israelite who sells himself to a sojourner may redeem himself or be redeemed, and, failing this, gains freedom in the year of jubilee. Yahweh's servants must not long serve others (Lev. 25:54-55).

Within the chosen community, both ritual and morality are rooted in the conception of Yahweh's holiness, a characteristic which is to be zealously emulated by His people whom He brought out of the land of Egypt. (Cf. Lev. 11: 45; 19: 36; 22: 32-33; 25: 38.)

Certain misdemeanors so greatly profane His holiness that for them the offender shall be "cut off from among his people."[2] Just how these guilty ones will be cut off by Yahweh is not

---

[2] These sins include failure to offer the blood of a slain animal as an oblation to Yahweh (Lev. 17: 3-4), offering a sacrifice without bringing it to the door of the tent of meeting (17: 8-9), eating any blood (17: 10), eating of a sacrifice after the second day (18: 7-8), giving children to Molech (20: 3), approaching hallowed things when ceremonially unclean (22: 3), and failure to afflict one's soul and refrain from all work on the Day of Atonement (23: 29). (The last point occurs in a section added by a priestly editor; cf. Brightman, *op. cit.*, p. 305; Bewer, *op. cit.*, p. 188.)

always specified; in some cases, however, they are to be put to death by the community.[3]

The spirit of all these penalties is summed up in the warning: "They shall therefore keep my charge, lest they bear sin for it, and die therein, if they profane it: I am Jehovah who sanctifieth them" (22:9).

To summarize, the holiness enjoined by this code is both ceremonial and ethical. Its ceremonial aspect deals with Israel's worship of Israel's God; its ethical aspect concerns the relations between Israelites and fellow-Israelites, sojourners being included in the community. The attitude of Israel toward foreign nations is apparently assumed to be one of hostility, since "enemies" are conveniently at hand to be conquered or submitted to, as Israel's obedience or disobedience may prompt Yahweh to decree. The emulation of Yahweh's holiness through obedience to His statutes is more precious to Him than the lives of His people; for both ritual and moral sins He may visit a death penalty upon individuals or upon the nation. And yet, despite the severity of His punishments, their ultimate purpose is the conversion of the nation to obedience and holiness and the enjoyment of His favor. Other nations may go their way. He may have power over them, but He does not care for them. He is Yahweh, the God of Israel.

LAMENTATIONS

In 586, Jerusalem was captured by the Babylonians, and most of the people of Judah were deported, amid the jeers of the Edomites who had sided with the Babylonians and shared in the plunder. The poems of lamentation which have been mistakenly attributed by tradition to the prophet Jeremiah arose out of the period following this calamity, possibly from some of the Jews still left in their devastated land.

The earliest of these lamentations seem to be chapters 2 and 4, written probably by the same person, who had experienced

[3] Such crimes are giving children to Molech (20:2), cursing father or mother (20:9), sexual sins (20:10-16), having a "familiar spirit" (20:27), blaspheming the name of Yahweh (24:16), and killing a man (24:21). Where indicated, the method is to be stoning.

the terror of the intercepted flight of King Zedekiah and his party (4:19-20), and the horror of the succeeding days of destruction and famine. This writer is so overwhelmed by the unspeakably dreadful condition of the people in Jerusalem that he hardly gets beyond the description of their horrible suffering and the reiteration of the conviction that it is all the pitiless smiting of Yahweh, who in wrath against Zion has become like an enemy.

> How hath the Lord covered the daughter of Zion with a cloud in his anger!
> He hath cast down from heaven unto the earth the beauty of Israel,
> And hath not remembered his footstool in the day of his anger.
>
> * * * * * *
>
> He hath bent his bow like an enemy, he hath stood with his right hand as an adversary,
> And hath slain all that were pleasant to the eye:
> In the tent of the daughter of Zion he hath poured out his wrath like fire. (2:1, 4; cf. 2:2-3, 5, 8, 17, 21-22; 4:11)

Even Yahweh's sanctuary, which His people had believed He would protect from profanation at all cost, has been ruthlessly destroyed by the heathen enemies. This must have happened through Yahweh's own ordering—surest proof of His all-consuming indignation! (2:7, 20c; 4:12) Now the best of Yahweh's people have been torn away from all that represents His presence in their environment (2:9bc).

Two other ideas, that sin in Israel is the cause of the wrath of Yahweh (4:13; 4:6, but cf. marginal reading), and that Yahweh may relent now that the chastisement has been inflicted (2:19), are suggested in these two poems, but not dwelt upon as they are in others written somewhat later, when the writers had recovered enough from the stunning blow to meditate upon its purpose and to reconcile it with their past fundamental conceptions of Yahweh. The latter idea is combined with the conviction that Yahweh will soon punish the hated Edomites who had rejoiced at Zion's downfall.

> The punishment of thine iniquity is accomplished, O daughter of Zion; he will no more carry thee away into captivity:
> He will visit thine iniquity, O daughter of Edom; he will uncover thy sins. (4:22)

Chapter 5 seems to come from a little later time than the lamentations that we have been considering. Here, the cause of all these calamities is clearly felt to be the sin, either of a former generation or of this one (5: 7, 16).

Yahweh is implored to remember the sufferings of the people, which in this case are not explicitly attributed to His direct destructive activity against them, but rather to His passivity while the "strangers" and "pursuers" worked havoc among them. He must have forsaken His people—and yet it seems as though after this long time of rejection He must be ready to show favor to them again. Is He still wroth with them? (5: 19-22)

In chapter 1, the sense of the nation's sin is still more prominent. Yahweh has Himself inflicted unparalleled woes upon the city "in the day of his fierce anger" (1: 12-15, 17). Yet this great suffering is, after all, but the just desert of a disobedient people.

> Jehovah is righteous; for I have rebelled against his commandment. (1:18a)
> Jerusalem hath grievously sinned; therefore she is become as an unclean thing. (1:8a; cf. 1:5ab, 20bc)

The most humiliating part of the situation is Zion's ignominious position among the other nations. Once she majestically ruled others; now she is subject to others, an object of derision (1:1, 3). Though formerly banned by Yahweh from His assembly, the nations have now thrust themselves into the sanctuary unhindered (1:10).

Those that have not actually overthrown Zion have rejoiced at her downfall. She is convinced that their time of reckoning with Yahweh is coming, and that He will punish their wickedness as He has punished hers.

> All mine enemies have heard of my trouble; they are glad that thou hast done it:
> Thou wilt bring the day that thou hast proclaimed, and they shall be like unto me.
> Let all their wickedness come before thee;
> And do unto them, as thou hast done unto me for all my transgressions. (1: 21bc-22ab)

Chapter 3, the latest of these poems, comes from one to whom the immediate horror of the situation is no longer present, and who can confidently expect Yahweh to have mercy soon.

As usual, the disaster is interpreted as directly purposed and inflicted by Yahweh in His wrath (3:1-3, 10-13). When thus resolved upon punishing, Yahweh is inexorable (3:8, 42-45).

Yet there is another side to Yahweh's character; He might have wiped them out entirely if His purpose had been solely punitive. He will be found at last to be merciful, if only men will wait patiently and hopefully. After all, Yahweh chastises only because men's sin forces Him to do it; why should one complain when he is receiving only what he deserves? Instead of blaming Yahweh, one should examine his own life and turn wholeheartedly to God, expectant of mercy (3:22-26, 30-33, 39-41). In anticipation of Yahweh's rescue from the present trouble, the poet cries with assurance, "Thou hast redeemed my life" (3:55-58).

But woe unto the enemy nations when Yahweh does turn to redeem His people! When He pays them back for their wrongs against Judah, His anger will work their destruction.

> Thou wilt render unto them a recompense, O Jehovah, according to the work of their hands.
> Thou wilt give them hardness of heart, thy curse unto them.
> Thou wilt pursue them in anger, and destroy them from under the heavens of Jehovah. (3:64-66)

In the book of Lamentations as a whole, we have found Yahweh to be a God of power and of righteousness, who, incensed at the sin of Judah, has brought upon her every conceivable calamity. Since it is probable that His wrath against Judah has been nearly appeased by her long-continued sufferings, and since He has been believed to be a God of mercy as well as a God of justice, there is some ground for hope that He will soon relent toward her, and turn the force of His indignant chastisement against Judah's enemies. Yahweh is still the God of one people, even though for a time they are suffering His active displeasure.

OTHER FRAGMENTS OF POETRY AND PROPHECY
FROM THE EXILIC PERIOD

ISAIAH 63:7 TO 64:12

The two prayers preserved in Isaiah 63:7-16 and 63:17 to 64:12 come from an unknown writer during the early years of the exilic period, living apparently in Palestine.[4]

Yahweh's attitude toward other nations is not explicitly described, but seems clearly implied. They do not share at all the relationship which has been Israel's high privilege. "Thy holy people" are contrasted with "our adversaries" who "have trodden down thy sanctuary" (63:18). The writer wishes that Yahweh would come with earthquake and fire "to make thy name known to thine adversaries, that the nations may tremble at thy presence!" (64:2b)

On the other hand, one of the most striking aspects of these prayers, except in this passage, is the writer's restraint. Considering the situation, they are amazingly free from vindictiveness toward enemies. This freedom from imprecation against present enemies is in harmony with the fact that in the reminiscence of Yahweh's gracious leading of Israel during the days of Moses (63:11-14) there is no mention of His confounding other nations in Israel's behalf.

Yahweh's attitude toward Israel in the present is interpreted from the nation's desolation. "Thou hast hid thy face from us, and hast consumed us by means of our iniquities" (64:7b). In the past, also, when the nation rebelled against Him, Yahweh "was turned to be their enemy, and himself fought against them" (63:10).

But such punishment is only a temporary phase of Yahweh's dealings with His people. By far the most prominent aspect of His attitude in the past has been lovingkindness and mercy, and this fills the writer with assurance of His redemptive love in the present. "I will make mention of the lovingkindness of Jehovah . . . and the great goodness toward the house of Israel, which he hath bestowed on them according to his mercies, and according to the multitude of his lovingkindnesses. For he said, Surely, they are my people, children that will not deal

[4] Cf. Bewer, *op. cit.*, p. 192.

falsely: so he was their Saviour. In all their affliction he was afflicted,[5] and the angel of his presence saved them: in his love and in his pity he redeemed them; and he bare them, and carried them all the days of old" (63:7-9). In spite of Yahweh's apparent displeasure, the same tender relationship must still be fundamentally real. "For thou art our Father, though Abraham knoweth us not, and Israel doth not acknowledge us: thou, O Jehovah, art our Father; our Redeemer from everlasting is thy name" (63:16; cf. 64:8).

Yahweh's methods are only vaguely suggested. In the past, He has led His people by His holy Spirit, and on occasion has manifested His presence by earthquake (63:11, 14; 64:3). Now, after their suffering, He is expected to help His people, since He is the only God ever known "who worketh for him that waiteth for him" (64:4b), but there is no description of the methods by which He will work, or the result for other nations.

In these prayers, then, we find Yahweh peculiarly the God, the Father, of this one nation, and we have remnants of old ideas about His dealings with men, but the omission of definite ideas of retaliation against adversaries may indicate an effort to spiritualize the conception of Yahweh's help to the nation. Significant, also, is the stress on His love and redemption rather than His anger toward Israel.

SONG OF MOSES (DEUTERONOMY 32)

From some unnamed poet of the exile comes the song attributed to Moses and found in Deuteronomy 32:1-43.

Yahweh is here "a God of faithfulness and without iniquity, just and right" (vs. 4), who has in time past been a "father" to His people (vs. 6) and watched over them with brooding care (vss. 10-14).

Israel, however, "lightly esteemed the Rock of his salvation" (vs. 15) and provoked Yahweh to anger and jealousy by unfaithfulness to Him (vss. 16-21). Incensed, He vowed to "heap evils upon them" (vss. 23-25). His impulse was to scatter them afar so that they would perish as a people, but, as in the thought

[5] This rendering of 63:9 a is based on a text later than the original one. Cf. Bewer, *op. cit.*, p. 193.

Writings from the Exilic Period 89

of Ezekiel, He was afraid that the nations might misinterpret His act, and say, "Our hand is exalted, and Jehovah hath not done all this" (vs. 27).

Hence, He, the all-powerful, who alone can kill and make alive, wound and heal (vs. 39), will "repent himself for his servants" (vs. 36), whet His glittering sword, and render vengeance to His adversaries (vss. 35, 41).

I will make mine arrows drunk with blood,
And my sword shall devour flesh;
With the blood of the slain and the captives,
From the head of the leaders of the people.
Rejoice, O ye nations, with his people:
For he will avenge the blood of his servants,
And will render vengeance to his adversaries.
And will make expiation for his land, for his people. (vss. 42-43)

Here, as so frequently, we find a God whose righteousness is demonstrated by His exercise of destructive might, first upon His own rebellious people, and then, still more fiercely, upon their enemies.

ISAIAH 13 AND 14:4-21

From 546 on, the victories of Cyrus offered to the exiled Jews in Babylonia an ever-increasing hope that the nation which had conquered them might itself be overthrown. In Isaiah 13 and 14:4-21, we have poems from one of their number, voicing their hatred for Babylon and their eager anticipation of her coming disaster.

"Jehovah of hosts is mustering the host for battle," coming, with "the weapons of his indignation, to destroy the whole land" (13:3-5). "The day of Jehovah cometh, cruel, with wrath and fierce anger" (13:9). The heavens and all the earth seem to be involved in the approaching catastrophe (13:10-13), when men shall be thrust through with the sword, their infants dashed in pieces, and their wives ravished (13:15-16, 18), but Yahweh's special target is Babylon, the mighty and beautiful city, soon to be made a desolate waste (13:19-22; 14:4-20, *passim*). Thus will Yahweh requite Babylon for the persecution of all the nations (14:6) and impious self-exaltation (14:12-15).

An editorial insertion (14:1-3) stresses the approaching comfort and restoration of the Jews, and rejoices that the tables will be turned—that "they shall take them captive whose captives they were; and they shall rule over their oppressors" (14:2).

These poems, we see, present the God of the Jews as preparing to bring horrible destruction upon the nation that has oppressed them and other nations.

ISAIAH 21:1-15

Another prophet of this period, living in Palestine, was experiencing terrifying visions through which Yahweh revealed to him the confusion and disaster coming upon Babylon (21:1-9).

Unlike the author of Isaiah 13-14, this seer does not dwell upon the fact of Yahweh's causing the destruction of the foe, nor does he indulge in vengeful exultation over Babylon. Moreover, toward Edom, the nation upon which so many Jews heaped execration, he seems to be friendly, answering as best he can the request from Edom for an interpretation of these momentous events (21:11-12). As for the Arabian caravans, he is concerned that in their flight "from the grievousness of war" they shall be provided with water and bread.[6]

Here, then, is a seer with a measure of international sympathy, who refrains from uttering words of hatred even against a doomed foe.

HISTORICAL WRITINGS WITH THE POINT OF VIEW OF DEUTERONOMY

KINGS

On the basis of material found in the Book of the Acts of Solomon and the royal annals kept in Israel and Judah, a historian who had been gripped by the dominant ideas of the deuteronomic code undertook, probably only a decade or two after Josiah's reformation in 621, to trace the history of the sister kingdoms in the light of these principles. This work, now found in I Kings 1 to II Kings 23:25a, was supplemented during the exile by another writer with the same point of view, who carried the story through the events of 586 and interpolated in the earlier writing indications of the coming tragedy. For our

[6] Cf. Bewer, *The Literature of the Old Testament*, pp. 197-199.

present purpose, we may treat these together, omitting, however, the Solomon stories, the Elijah and Elisha cycles, and the history of the rise and fall of the house of Omri, all of which have previously been discussed.

Consistently with the thought of Deuteronomy and contemporary prophets, Yahweh is "the God of Israel," but is also supreme over all the kingdoms of the earth (II K. 19:14-19). He uses other nations, controlling the movements of the Assyrians and then at length, to save Jerusalem, sending His angel to smite nearly two thousand of them (II K. 19, *passim*), and later sending Chaldeans, Syrians, Moabites, and Ammonites against Jerusalem (II K. 24:2; cf. II K. 15:37).

Various strange acts are attributed to Yahweh, under the conviction that every striking occurrence is purposed by Him. Rehoboam's unresponsiveness to the people's demand for redress of grievances is "a thing brought about of Jehovah, that he might establish his word" spoken through Ahijah to Jeroboam (I K. 12:15, 24). Though Yahweh quite approved of Jehu, in his days He "began to cut off from Israel: and Hazael smote them in all the borders of Israel" (II K. 10:32), and oppression by Syria continued until the time of Joash, but "Jehovah was gracious" unto Israel then, and gave them "a saviour" from the Syrians (II K. 13:3-5, 22-25) eventually restoring all their territory under the wicked Jeroboam II (II K. 14:25-27). In other words, these things happened then, and so this writer says that Yahweh did them, without being quite so concerned as the Chronicler is later, to work out a complete correspondence between apparent desert and Yahweh's treatment. Similarly, Azariah's leprosy means that "Jehovah smote the king," even though no reason is given (II K. 15:5).

In spite of some of these unexplained cases, the author's general theory is that, as Deuteronomy promises, obedience to Yahweh's statutes is rewarded and disobedience is punished. The chief sin in Yahweh's eyes is the debased worship at other sanctuaries than Jerusalem. The captivity of Israel is punishment for having "feared other gods, and walked in the statutes of the nations, whom Jehovah cast out from before the children of Israel, and of the kings of Israel, which they made"—building "high places," burning incense there, and serving idols (II K. 17:7-23). "Therefore Jehovah was very angry with Israel, . . . and delivered them into the hand of spoilers, until he had cast them out of his sight." The kings who foster such sins are threatened with grievous retribution. All of Jeroboam's line must be cut off by horrible deaths (I K. 14:7-11; 15:29-30), and a similar fate is decreed for Baasha and others (I K. 16:3, 12, 18-19). For Manasseh's abominations, Yahweh "will wipe Jerusalem as a man wipeth a dish" (II K. 21:10-15).

The idea that such disloyalty provokes Yahweh to anger is constantly repeated (e.g., I K. 14:9, 15; 15:30; 16:2, 7, 13, 26; etc.). Even foreigners settled in His land must fear Him, and when the colonists brought into Samaria after 722 fail to show this fear, He sends lions among them (II K. 17:25).

Any king who wiped out contaminating influences from Yahweh's religion and led the people into more loyal obedience to Him would naturally be highly approved. Such are Hezekiah, who, for removing the high places and the idols, is enabled by Yahweh to rebel against Assyria and to conquer the Philistines (II K. 18:3-8), and Josiah, who heeds the words of the law book found in the Temple and institutes a thoroughgoing reformation (II K. 22:1 to 23:25). In the northern kingdom, none of the kings could meet the test of worship at Jerusalem, but Jehu, having slain all the line of Ahab and all the worshippers of Baal, is praised by Yahweh in the strongest terms: "Because thou hast done well in executing that which is right in mine eyes, and hast done unto the house of Ahab according to all that was in my heart, thy sons of the fourth generation shall sit on the throne of Israel!" (II K. 10:30)

One of the important things to be found in the annals of a great king is "all his might," and sometimes also "how he warred" (I K. 15:23; 16:5, 27; II K. 10:34; 13:8, 12; 14:28). Wars are prominent throughout the story, as we have already had occasion to discover in the discussion of other points. Sometimes Yahweh is said to be controlling them, sometimes they are noted without explicit reference to His part in them (e.g., I K. 14:30; 15:6, 7, 16, 32). We scarcely need to give evidence that lives of other peoples are not of equal value with those of Israelites, for we should not expect to find them so regarded. We may notice one striking instance, where within the nation Amaziah's blood revenge for his father is punctiliously limited to the murderers themselves, and in the succeeding verse, with no provocation stated, "he slew of Edom in the Valley of Salt ten thousand" (II K. 14:5-7).

We have seen that in the books of Kings we have a conception of God's control of all nations built upon the thought of the pre-exilic writing prophets. As in their conception, Yahweh is not now a God who fights with His own people against another nation supported by its own god, but the one God who brings either victory or defeat upon His own special people according as their obedience or disloyalty may deserve. His one concern is for them to obey His requirements as given in Deuteronomy, with emphasis on the demand for worship at Jerusalem alone. Other nations serve as means of reward or punishment, but do not count for anything in themselves.

D FRAMEWORK OF JUDGES

We have previously discussed the sections of Judges that are akin to the J and E documents, so we shall now need to glance at only the deuteronomistic framework in which these earlier writings were set. It was probably during the exile that writers with religious conceptions similar to those of the author of Kings retouched all the earlier historical writings. Except in Deuteronomy itself, their work is most prominent in Judges.

The D writer carries out more completely E's idea of the people's apostasy and oppressions and the nation-wide significance of the judges. The spontaneity and individualism and vivid coloring of the heroic deeds of that rough age are here lost in the impression of an inevitably recurring cycle of national experience. The people worship other gods and provoke Yahweh to anger; for punishment, He sells them into the hands of some enemy nation; for a definite period they are oppressed by this conqueror; then Yahweh answers Israel's cry for help by raising up a "judge" who delivers the whole people and then "judges" them as a sort of theocratic deputy; under his good influence, they serve Yahweh again, but with his death a new cycle begins with apostasy from His worship. (Cf. 2:11-12,

14-15, 18-19; 3:7-15; 4:1-4; 6:1-6; 8:27b-28, 33-35; 13:1; 15:20.)

During the period treated in Judges, there was of course no central sanctuary, Jerusalem being still in the hands of the Jebusites, so the deuteronomists could not here bring out Yahweh's requirement of centralized worship, but in other respects the idea of Yahweh is like that found in Kings.

DEUTERO-ISAIAH

One of the Jewish exiles in Babylon, a poet of deep religious sensitiveness, became assured that Yahweh's hand was directing the movements of Cyrus, in order to free His people from captivity, and he summoned his fellow-captives to joyous preparation for the deliverance that would soon be wrought for them. Though this man, in certain of his poems, uttered one of the most unusual and challenging messages ever given to mankind, his work was not preserved under his own name, but became attached to the book of Isaiah, as chapters 40 to 55, and is commonly referred to as Deutero-Isaiah.

Besides making a unique contribution, which will be treated later, Deutero-Isaiah conserves and develops further many of the ideas of former prophets.

Yahweh's creative power and present omnipotence in nature, though not a new idea, is here the theme of such majestic passages that the reader realizes in a fresh way His absolute control (40:12; 42:5; 44:24; 45:7, 12, 18). In comparison with Him, men are as insignificant as grasshoppers (40:22-24), and the nations that think themselves so great are like "a drop of a bucket" or "the small dust of the balance"—"less than nothing, and vanity" (40:15-17). Chariots and armies are "quenched as a wick" (43:17).

These considerations support the constantly repeated claim that Yahweh is the only God in the universe, the everlasting God, the One who has had foreknowledge of everything from the beginning, who has ordered the cosmos entirely alone, "the first and the last" (e.g., 40:28; 43:10-11; 44:6-8; 46:9-10). He alone can "make peace, and create evil" (45:7). It is ridiculous to think of an idol as anything but a piece of lifeless wood or stone, utterly futile and senseless (40:19-20; 41:7, 21-24, 29; 42:8, 17; 44:9-11; 45:20; 46:1, 5-7).

As Deutero-Isaiah thus carries to their furthest limit the monotheistic ideas of some of his predecessors, so also he deals with his second ancient theme, Yahweh's special relation to Israel, with a beauty and thorough-going consistency hardly matched by any other writer.

Yahweh is not only the Creator of heaven and earth—He is in a very intimate way "the Holy One of Israel" (e.g., 41:14, 20; 43:3, 14; 54:5), or even "the King of Jacob" (41:21; cf. 43:15; 44:6). He has in a special way created or "formed" Israel (e.g., 43:1; 44:2, 21).

Yahweh is a God who punishes His people's iniquity, even in fierce anger (42:24-25; 43:27-28), but afterwards He pardons and restores—and it is almost solely the latter phase of the divine attitude that this prophet of the exile longs to portray to his disheartened countrymen. "I have blotted out, as a thick cloud, thy transgressions, and, as a cloud, thy sins: return unto me, for I have redeemed thee" (44:22). "For a small moment have I forsaken thee; but with great mercies will I gather thee. In overflowing wrath I hid my face from thee for a moment; but with everlasting lovingkindness will I have mercy on thee, saith Jehovah thy Redeemer" (54:7-8). (Cf. 40:2; 43:24*b*-25; 51:17-23; 55:6-7.) The Redeemer of His people—this is Yahweh's most prominent rôle (e.g., 41:14; 43:1, 14; 44:6, 22-24).

Being all-powerful, Yahweh is absolutely free to choose whatever instrument He will to carry out His purposes. To redeem Israel, He has called Cyrus, and endowed him with power to subdue the nations. "I have raised him up in righteousness, and I will make straight all his ways: he shall build my city, and he shall let my exiles go free" (45:13; cf. 41:2, 25; 44:28; 45:1-4; 46:10-11; 48:14-15).

Yahweh's marvelous care for His people, His constant regard for their need, His miraculous preparations for their safe return to their land and His promise of food and drink and protection all the way, are celebrated in unforgettable passages throughout these poems. (Cf. 40:27; 41:17; 42:16; 43:1-2, 5-7, 20; 44: 3-5; 46:3-4; 48:17-21; 49:8-13; 51:1-3, 16; 52:12, 55:1-5,

12-13.) His love finds expression occasionally in words of even deeper tenderness. "Can a woman forget her sucking child, that she should not have compassion on the son of her womb? yea, these may forget, yet will not I forget thee. Behold, I have graven thee upon the palms of my hands" (49:15-16a; cf. 54:10; 40:11).

The combined ideas of Yahweh's power and His love for Israel lead sometimes to an exaltation of the might that will be used on her behalf. "Jehovah will go forth as a mighty man; he will stir up his zeal like a man of war: he will cry, yea, he will shout aloud; he will do mightily against his enemies" (42:13; cf. 40:10; 51:9).

The conception of the discomfiture of Israel's enemies, so necessary a part, evidently, of the thought of restoration, appears occasionally even in Deutero-Isaiah. "They that war against thee shall be as nothing" (cf. 41:11-12, 15). The Redeemer and Holy One of Israel will take vengeance upon Babylon for merciless oppression of His people, temporarily given over into her hand (ch. 47; cf. 49:25-26; 51:22-23). Elsewhere, Israel is magnified at the expense of other nations in general, rather than just Babylon. Other peoples will be given as a ransom for Israel's life (43:3-4); the Egyptians, Ethiopians, and Sabeans will come in chains as suppliants, recognizing that God is in Israel only—while Israel herself "shall be saved by Jehovah with an everlasting salvation" (45:14-17); she will be brought back to her land by the nations, kings and queens licking the dust of her feet (49:22-23). After Zion's restoration, "no weapon that is formed against thee shall prosper" (54:15-17).

Such ideas as these might be matched by passages from many other exilic and post-exilic writings, and if they represented Deutero-Isaiah's dominant thought, we should not accord him any place of peculiar importance. The use of Yahweh's great power for the exaltation of His chosen people is an old story; this prophet's unique contribution is a conception really contradictory to the one just discussed, a new solution of the problem created by Yahweh's universal power but special love.

According to this new conception, Yahweh purposes that righteousness and salvation shall reach the very ends of the earth (45:8; 51:4-7). He has, indeed, chosen Israel as His beloved, but as a "servant"—not merely for Israel's own sake, but rather to be the means of giving the true religion to all the nations, near and far, that they may know and worship Yahweh (49:6; cf. 45:22-23). Israel's mission is to "bring forth justice [or a universal moral religion] to the Gentiles," (42:1-4); to be "a light of the Gentiles, to open the blind eyes, to bring out the prisoners from the dungeon, and them that sit in darkness out of the prison-house" (42:6-7). In the longest of the "servant poems," 52:13 to 53:12, the other nations are represented as actually recognizing and accepting the salvation mediated to them through Israel.

Yet, remarkable as is this thought of Israel's mission to the whole world, the method of its accomplishment is even more astonishing. Israel's *suffering* is to bring the salvation of the nations! The servant's quiet suffering and non-resistance are portrayed in a number of passages. "He will not cry, nor lift up his voice, nor cause it to be heard in the street" (42:2). "He was despised, and rejected of men; a man of sorrows, and acquainted with grief" (53:3a). "He was oppressed, yet when he was afflicted he opened not his mouth; as a lamb that is led to the slaughter, and as a sheep before her shearers is dumb, so he opened not his mouth" (53:7). At last the other nations realize in amazement that this one whom they thought to be smitten by God as a punishment has in fact been suffering for their sake. "Surely he hath borne our griefs, and carried our sorrows; ... he was wounded for our transgressions, he was bruised for our iniquities; the chastisement of our peace was upon him; and with his stripes we are healed" (53:4-5; cf, vss. 6, 10, 12). Such an unprecedented method will prove effectual! The nations *will* be won by vicarious suffering: "He shall see of the travail of his soul, and shall be satisfied: by the knowledge of himself shall my righteous servant justify many; and he shall bear their iniquities" (53:11).

Here, then, is a new principle of life. The suffering of a nation, instead of being avenged by force, is to be borne without resistance and *used*—used as a means of redeeming even the nations that have caused the suffering. Yahweh has purposed this (53:10)—it is His method of bringing the nations to know Him. The "suffering servant poems" offer on the one hand a new explanation of suffering—on the other hand, and more important for this study, a wholly new conception of the way to international influence.

We have seen that Deutero-Isaiah carried over or developed further many ideas started by his predecessors, adopted by his successors, and familiar to-day as important elements in religious thought—particularly, monotheism and the idea of the tender divine care for those whom God loves. In his conception of a nation serving through suffering, however, and winning the world with this paradoxical kind of power, this prophet had no predecessor—and neither his own nation nor any other has ever wholeheartedly ventured on the possibility of the truth of his conception.[7]

Cf. Cadbury, *National Ideals in the Old Testament*, pp. 199-205.

CHAPTER VI

WRITINGS FROM THE FIRST CENTURY AFTER THE RESTORATION

1. Prophetic Work in the Early Restoration Period—2. The P Document—3. Further Prophetic Work—4. Memoirs of Nehemiah and of Ezra—5. Ruth

PROPHETIC WORK IN THE EARLY RESTORATION PERIOD

HAGGAI

After the return of a group of the Jews to their own land in 538 B.C., the glorious prophetic hopes of triumphant prestige and unexampled prosperity failed to be realized, and the community in and about Jerusalem became utterly disheartened. Their crops were failing, their people were few and insignificant, their neighbors were hostile—and altogether the Jews had little spirit for undertaking the great task of rebuilding the ruined Temple. In 520 Haggai arose, seconded by Zechariah, to spur the people on and point out to them the reason for their miserable condition.

The Yahweh of Haggai is in control of nature, and has been using His power to withhold prosperity from His people until they rebuild His house (1:9-11). During the time of their indifference to this project, He has apparently not been "with them," but now that they are undertaking it, "Be strong . . . and work: for I am with you, saith Jehovah of hosts" (2:4b; cf. 1:13).

With His favor now directed toward them, Yahweh's attitude becomes more significant for our present study. His control of nature which has brought them dearth before will now bring marvelous prosperity, but not only physical nature is to be "shaken" for the glorification of Yahweh's house and His chosen

100 *The God of the Old Testament in Relation to War*

people. He is about to overthrow all nations with a tremendous destruction, to the end that His chosen ones may be exalted. "Yet once, it is a little while, and I will shake the heavens, and the earth, . . . and I will shake all nations; and the precious things of all nations shall come; and I will fill this house with glory, saith Jehovah of hosts" (2: 6-7).[1] "Speak to Zerubbabel, governor of Judah, saying, I will shake the heavens and the earth; and I will overthrow the throne of kingdoms; and I will destroy the strength of the kingdoms of the nations; and I will overthrow the chariots, and those that ride in them; and the horses and their riders shall come down, every one by the sword of his brother. In that day, saith Jehovah of hosts, will I take thee, O Zerubbabel, my servant, the son of Shealtiel, saith Jehovah, and will make thee as a signet; for I have chosen thee, saith Jehovah of hosts" (2: 21-23).

According to Haggai, then, Yahweh cares supremely for His people's regard for His temple. Given that, He will overthrow the other nations through war, and make Judah, under its Davidic prince, supreme over all.

ZECHARIAH

Two months after the beginning of Haggai's prophetic work, a very different personality joined the effort to fire Yahweh's people with the assurance of His presence and aid, and so to stimulate them to carry to completion the task of rebuilding the Temple. The allegorical, apocalyptic vision is Zechariah's most characteristic literary form, though not all of his message is so expressed.

To Zechariah, Yahweh is omnipotent and is in touch with every part of the earth. The prophet sees heavenly horsemen "whom Jehovah hath sent to walk to and fro through the earth" and report upon conditions everywhere (1: 10-11; cf. 6: 5-7),

---

[1] Cf. Mitchell, H. G., *International Critical Commentary* on *Haggai*, p. 62, for the interpretation that these "precious things of all nations" will be voluntary offerings to the Temple from the nations liberated by the great political convulsion of the world and "so impressed by the power of Yahweh that they would recognize Him as the Ruler of the world."

and later he is shown the symbols for "the eyes of Jehovah, which run to and fro through the whole earth" (4:10b).

This all-seeing, all-powerful Yahweh has in the past been "sore displeased" with His people for not heeding the words of the prophets and turning from their evil ways (1:2-6; 7:9-14; 8:14). In response, however, to the angel's query, "O Jehovah of hosts, how long wilt thou not have mercy on Jerusalem and on the cities of Judah, against which thou hast had indignation these threescore and ten years?" (1:12) Yahweh reveals that now His purpose for His people is wholly beneficent. "I am jealous for Jerusalem and for Zion with a great jealousy. . . . I am returned to Jerusalem with mercies; my house shall be built in it. . . . My cities shall overflow with prosperity; and Jehovah shall yet comfort Zion, and shall yet choose Jerusalem" (1:14, 16-17; cf. 2:12-13; 8:2-3, 7-8). The restored remnant is "a brand plucked out of the fire" (3:2b), and, in the person of the high priest Joshua, is pronounced cleansed (3:4).[2]

The new city will have no need of walls for fortification, "for I, saith Jehovah, will be unto her a wall of fire round about, and I will be the glory in the midst of her" (2:5). Likewise, it is solely through divine spiritual force that Zerubbabel is to accomplish his destined work: "Not by might, nor by power, but by my Spirit, saith Jehovah of hosts" (4:6b).

Yahweh's purpose for His own people has as its corollaries two quite distinct ideas with regard to other nations.

On the one hand, Yahweh is "very sore displeased" with the nations that have afflicted His people more severely than He had desired (1:15). "The horns which have scattered Judah, Israel, and Jerusalem" will be overwhelmed by the four smiths (1:19-21). Yahweh will deal with "the nations that plundered you; for he that toucheth you toucheth the apple of his eye . . . and they shall be a spoil to those that served them" (2:8-9a).

On the other hand, occasionally when thinking of the nations in general, rather than the specific enemies of the Jews, the

[2] The ethical requirements for the restored community are explicitly given (8:16-17). Further emphasis on the moral reformation of Yahweh's people is given in the vision of the "flying roll" with its magically efficacious curse for all who steal or swear (5:3-4), and the expulsion of the woman who personifies wickedness, who is sealed in an ephah and borne away "to build her a house in the land of Shinar!" (5:7-11) Evidently, it is not particularly displeasing to Yahweh for wickedness to flourish in Babylonia, as long as Judah is cleansed.

prophet grasps a remarkably universalistic conception. Though Yahweh will still have His special dwelling in Zion, many nations will come to share in His worship, and will even belong to Him— will become His people (2:11; 6:15a; 8:22). "In those days it shall come to pass, that ten men shall take hold, out of all the languages of the nations, they shall take hold of the skirt of him that is a Jew, saying, We will go with you, for we have heard that God is with you" (8:23).

Zechariah, then, pictures an all-powerful God who at present purposes to shower blessings upon His restored people and to dwell with them in the Temple which they are rebuilding. The nations that have worked havoc with them will be cast down— but in the ideal future day Yahweh will be worshipped by many other nations besides the Jews. He is not an impartial God, but outsiders will one day be admitted to the group that He favors.

ISAIAH 56-66, PASSIM (NOT TRITO-ISAIAH)

It seems that the message now found in Isaiah 56:9 to 58:12; 59:1-15a; 65:1-16; and 66:1-6, 15-18a, 24 [3] probably comes from the period during which Haggai and Zechariah were convincing the Jewish community that Yahweh was greatly concerned to have His house rebuilt. The writer of these passages has a different conception of Yahweh's primary requirement, without the fulfillment of which He cannot dwell effectively among His people. With heaven as His throne and earth as His footstool, Yahweh cannot need this house that they are building (66:1-2a), nor care for the animal sacrifices that some deem so important to Him (66:3) nor for their ceremonial fasts (58:3-5).

Yahweh has just one kind of requirement—a contrite spirit and fear of His word (57:15; 66:2b, 5), resulting in a life of righteousness and kindness—"to loose the bonds of wickedness . . . and let the oppressed go free," to give bread to the hungry, to clothe the naked, and to take in the homeless poor (58:6-7, 9b-10). Such is the conduct that will make Yahweh

---

[3] Cf. Bewer, *The Literature of the Old Testament*, p. 242.

hear their cry, and guide them, and give them prosperity (58: 8-9a, 11-12).

He earnestly desires to have His people turn to Him with such service. "I have spread out my hands all the day unto a rebellious people" (65:2). He is ready to hear and save, "but your iniquities have separated between you and your God, and your sins have hid his face from you, so that he will not hear" (59: 1-2). He wants to heal and give peace (57:17-19).

However, much as He may desire to bless a loyal people, as a whole they are utterly disloyal—idolatrous (57:3-10), and morally wicked in every imaginable way (58:1; 59:3, 7-14). "There is no peace, saith my God, to the wicked" (57:12). This God who would have liked to heal "will come with fire . . . to render his anger with fierceness . . . For by fire will Jehovah execute judgment, and by his sword, upon all flesh; and the slain of Jehovah shall be many" (66:15-16; cf. 66:6, 24; 65:12, 15). He will discriminate between His servants and the wicked, giving food and drink and joy to the righteous, and the opposite to the wicked (65:13-14).

Almost in the tone of the pre-exilic prophets, we have here a God of righteousness whose people as a whole are either willfully wicked or mistaken in their conception of what is pleasing to Him. He will abundantly bless those who respond to His overtures and live in god-fearing righteousness, but He must vex and slay the sinful.

This may be a suitable place to note Isaiah 56:1-8, the passage just preceding this unknown prophet's work—though its stress on the sabbath and the Temple service precludes the possibility of its coming from the same person.

This is noteworthy as a protest against the policy of Ezekiel and his followers, who desired to exclude all foreigners from participation in even the menial parts of the Temple ministry. This writer believes that Yahweh wants His house to be called "a house of prayer for all peoples," and that "the Lord Jehovah, who gathereth the outcasts of Israel, saith, Yet will I gather others to him, besides his own that are gathered'' (56:7b-8). Foreigners that love Yahweh and serve Him loyally will be acceptable ministers in His house of prayer (56:6-7a). A phrase from this nameless prophet of generous tolerance was found adequate to express Jesus' conception of the Temple (Mk. 11:17).

TRITO-ISAIAH

The prophet whose utterances are preserved in Isaiah 59:15b to 63:6; 65:17-25; and 66:7-14. 18b-23 [4] sounds like a disciple of Deutero-Isaiah, clinging to his glorious hopes of marvelous joy and divine blessing for the Jews, even amid the discouraging actual conditions of the restored community. The mission of "Trito-Isaiah," as he is called, was to try to revive in his compatriots such an enthusiastic hope that their faith in Yahweh could surmount the bleak present.

Many of the favorite phrases of Deutero-Isaiah reappear in these poems. The "Holy One of Israel," "Saviour," "Redeemer," "Mighty One of Jacob" (59:20; 60:8, 14, 16) purposes for His people "salvation" and "righteousness" (60:17b-18, 21; 61:10-11; 62:1, 11-12). This prophet's mission is "to preach good tidings to the meek; . . . to bind up the brokenhearted, to proclaim liberty to the captives, and the opening of the prison to them that are bound; to proclaim the year of Jehovah's favor"—and—"the day of vengeance of our God" 61:1-2). Apparently only the sad and imprisoned spirits among the Jews are to be the objects of his ministry, rather than the Gentiles, as in the similar passage from Deutero-Isaiah (42:6-7).

Glory and joy are in store for Jerusalem, upon whom Yahweh's light will shine while darkness is over all the rest of the earth (60:1-2; cf. 60:17-22; 65:17-23; 66:10-14). Yahweh will answer His people before they call (65:24), and will tame even the wild animals in the coming happy day, somewhat as in the vision of the first Isaiah (65:25). The whole earth will realize Yahweh's glory (66:18b-19) and recognize Zion's wondrous blessing at His hand (60:3; 61:9).

What this favor for Zion involves for the other nations is elsewhere worked out more fully. All nations will give up their precious things to enhance her glory and prosperity (60:5-9,

[4] Cf. Bewer, *op. cit.*, p. 246.

16; 61:6-7). Further, they will be actually subject to the "Zion of the Holy One of Israel." "Foreigners shall build up thy walls, and their kings shall minister unto thee . . . For that nation that will not serve thee shall perish . . . and all they that despised thee shall bow themselves down at the soles of thy feet" (60:10-14). "Foreigners" will be shepherds and plowmen and vinedressers for the Jews, while they themselves will be the privileged class, "priests of Jehovah" (61:5-6).

To accomplish this exaltation of His people, Yahweh is occasionally described as a mighty warrior. The note of divine "vengeance" found among the compassionate elements in the prophet's commission (61:2) now appears in its full significance. With "righteousness as a breastplate," "a helmet of salvation," "garments of vengeance for clothing," and "zeal as a mantle," He "will repay, wrath to his adversaries, recompense to his enemies" (59:17-18). In another passage, Yahweh comes from Edom, His garments dyed red with the blood of the peoples that He has wrathfully trodden as in a winepress. He asserts that, with "none to help," "I trod down the peoples in mine anger, and made them drunk in my wrath, and I poured out their lifeblood on the earth" (63:1-6). Verily, "he will have indignation against his enemies" (66:14c), and it is small wonder that the whole earth will fear the name of Yahweh (59:19).

It thus becomes evident that this disciple has caught Deutero-Isaiah's assurance of a coming glorious restoration for Yahweh's people, and his eagerness for righteousness as well as salvation, for Israel. However, in his conception of the effect of Zion's experience upon other nations, he has grasped only the hope of national exaltation and dominion, leaving out the really unique ideas of the former prophet—Yahweh's purpose to redeem the Gentiles, and to use as His mediator to them a patiently suffering servant-nation. In his thought of what constitutes a nation's greatness, Trito-Isaiah was not ahead of most of the people of his own time, or of ours.

In connection with Trito-Isaiah, we may consider the prophecy in Isaiah 34-35, which bears so many similarities to his thought.

Here the blind and the deaf and the lame and the dumb (among the Jews) will be restored, to respond to the joy of the march of the redeemed along "the way of holiness" back to Zion (35: 5-10; cf. vss. 1-2).

Much as with Trito-Isaiah, the message is a combination of favor for Zion and vengeance upon other nations. "Be strong, fear not: behold, your God will come with vengeance, with the recompense of God; he will come and save you" (35: 4). Though in Yahweh's "day of vengeance, a year of recompense for the cause of Zion" (34: 8) all nations will be slaughtered, and the mountains melted with their blood (34: 2-3), still, as in Trito-Isaiah's thought, the chief object of His destructive wrath will be Edom. His sword is filled with blood from his "great slaughter" there, and He has made the land pitch and brimstone, burning forever, with wild beasts and birds of prey for its only inhabitants (34: 5-15).

Thus, here again a prophet's theme is joyous salvation for Zion, with other nations subdued by vengeful divine might.

The P Document

The legal development to which Ezekiel and the author of the Holiness Code had contributed reached a still further stage in the Priest Code, or P document, formulated about 500 B.C. by some of the Jews who had remained in Babylonia.

The God of the priestly document is a transcendent Being. His will bears all before it, and we feel no such realistic struggle with intractable human wills, no such trial-and-error method in the government of the universe, as J presents.

The greatest interest of this document is the ceremonial approach to God. The function of the priesthood, and all the cultic institutions of Judaism, are central in the thought of the writers, and dominate their view of history.

Such ideas of God and of religion tend to throw emphasis upon matters that are hardly relevant to this investigation, but still there are many significant indications of God's attitude toward His own people and toward other peoples.

Since the P document begins with creation, God deals for a

time with all humanity, before His choice of Abraham and his seed for a special covenant relationship with Him. "God created man in his own image, in the image of God created he him; male and female created he them" (Gen. 1:27). Because of the corruption of "all flesh," except Noah, they must all be destroyed (Gen. 6:13, 17-18*a*). After the flood, God establishes, through Noah, a covenant with all flesh not to destroy them again by a flood, making the rainbow the covenant token (Gen. 9:11, 17).

The genealogies of other nations besides Israel are of interest to the priestly writers. The "generations of the sons of Noah" include Japheth (Gen. 10:2-5) and Ham, "after their families, after their tongues, in their lands, in their nations" (Gen. 10: 6-7, 20), as well as Shem, the ancestor of the Hebrews. The generations of Ishmael are given briefly (Gen. 25:12-16), and the descendants of Esau are recorded at great length (Gen. 36: 1-30, 40-43).

In addressing Yahweh, Moses twice calls Him "the God of the spirits of all flesh" (Num. 16:22; 27:16).

With the slight exceptions indicated above, the Creator of the universe and His priestly interpreters apparently limit their interest to the welfare of the seed of Abraham.

El Shaddai, or God Almighty,[5] covenants with Abraham to make him the father of a multitude of nations, to establish an everlasting covenant with his seed, to be their God, and to give them the whole land of Canaan for an everlasting possession (Gen. 17:4, 6-8, 10). This promise is reinforced by Yahweh's words to Abraham regarding Sarah and Isaac (Gen. 17:16).. Ishmael, being also a son of Abraham, will have a great posterity, but the covenant relationship is reserved for Isaac (Gen. 17: 18-21). When Jacob is about to depart for Paddan-aram, Isaac invokes for him the covenant blessing (Gen. 28:3-4), and later El Shaddai Himself appears to Jacob at Beth-el and confirms it (Gen. 35:11-12). Before his death, Jacob tells Joseph of this divine promise, and at the time of His revelation of His name "Yahweh," God tells Moses that He is now about to fulfill His covenant with the patriarchs (Ex. 6:4, 8).

[5] An epithet which accords well with the view of God throughout this document, though it is used only in revelations to the patriarchs, before the name Yahweh is revealed to Moses; cf. Gen. 17:1; 28:3; 35:11; 48:3; Ex. 6:2-3.

Although it does not indicate a new covenant, Yahweh's giving the sabbath as a "sign between me and you throughout your generations; that ye may know that I am Jehovah who sanctifieth you" (Ex. 31:13) is a strengthening of that bond with His people which the covenant represents.

Besides the establishment of His covenant, or as the result of it, Yahweh performs many gracious acts for His people.

For Abraham's sake, He saves Lot from the doomed city of Sodom (Gen. 19:29).

He takes knowledge of the Egyptian oppression, and, remembering His covenant, promises rescue (Ex. 1:13-14; 2:23b-25; 6:5-7). On the Passover night, He accomplishes their deliverance (Ex. 12:41-42a). During the wilderness journey, Yahweh provides quails and manna (Ex. 16:12), and the supply of food does not stop until the produce of their new land meets their need (Josh. 5:12). Throughout their journeying, He leads them by the cloud and the fire (Ex. 40:38).

Yahweh bids: "Let them make me a sanctuary, that I may dwell among them" (Ex. 25:8), and He graciously makes provision for their access to Him (e.g., Ex. 28:29; 29:43-46).

Many of the provisions of the cult suggest Yahweh's gracious or merciful attitude toward His people. A way is given for expiating unwitting sin (Lev. 4:1-5; 13). Either the congregation or an individual may obtain forgiveness for such sin (Num. 15:22, 24-25a, 27-28). One may atone for wrong dealings with other men (Lev. 6:1-7), and for sins of various kinds (Num. 5:6-7). The poor may bring less expensive sin-offerings than the usual ones (Lev. 5:7-13). As in other law codes, cities of refuge are established for the manslayer who kills by accident and without enmity (Num. 35:10-15, 22-28; Josh. 20:1-3, 7-9). Perhaps the most picturesque of the provisions for restoration to a right relationship with Yahweh is the ceremony on the Day of Atonement (cf. Lev. 16:9-10, 21-22, 29-30).

Frequently, it is stipulated that there shall be a uniform law for the sojourner and for the home-born. So, for instance, a sojourner who has been circumcised may keep the Passover (Ex. 12:48-49; Num. 9:14), there shall be one law for both regarding offerings (Num. 15:14-16), and regarding atonement for unwitting sin (Num. 15:29).

It will be observed that these gracious acts recorded by the priestly writers are practically all either common incidents in Hebrew historical narrative, by no means unique in this document, or else precautions to prevent Yahweh's people from being destroyed for violating the requirements—chiefly cultic requirements—of His sanctity.

No eager, seeking love pulsates through these stereotyped narratives and these ritual devices for cleansing from "sin" which has been committed through innocent accident. To show that "I am Jehovah" is evidently the purpose of the greater part of God's activity.

That the people had great need of some means of escape from the terrible consequences of "sin" is shown by a glance at the punishments inflicted by Yahweh.

Nadab and Abihu, the sons of Aaron, are devoured by fire from Yahweh for offering "strange fire" before Him (Lev. 10: 1-3a; cf. Num. 3:4; 26:61). Danger of death awaits the priests at every turn unless they scrupulously observe every ceremonial precaution against profanation (Lev. 10:6-9; 16:2).

On account of the people's murmuring and faithless fear before entering the promised land, that generation must die in the wilderness (Num. 14:26-30, 36-37; Num. 26:64-65). Later, this punishment of the people's faintheartedness is used as a warning and incentive for Gad and Reuben to help the other tribes invade the West-Jordan territory (Num. 32:6-8, 10a, 14-15).

For Korah's rebellion against Moses and Aaron, centering in the presumptuous and sacrilegious offering of incense by Korah and his company, two hundred and fifty men are consumed by fire from Yahweh (Num. 16:20-24, 35, 39-40). Then for the people's murmuring against Moses and Aaron and saying, "Ye have killed the people of Jehovah," Yahweh wants to consume them all; ritual atonement halts the plague that Yahweh sends, but not until nearly fifteen thousand persons have died (Num. 16:41, 45-49).

Sometimes, the penalty for wrongdoing is to be "cut off" from the chosen people. Such a punishment is visited upon the uncircumcised male (Gen. 17:14) or the person who commits sin intentionally (Num. 15:30-31).

The explicit death penalty is much more frequent. It must be inflicted upon one who breaks the sabbath (Ex. 35:2), and a specific example of the observance of this law is given when a man is stoned to death by the congregation for gathering sticks on the sabbath (Num. 15:32-36). The principle of "blood for blood" is enunciated after the flood (Gen. 9:5-6), and the law of blood revenge is elaborated further in another part of the code (Num. 35:19, 31, 33-34). Blood "polluteth the land" (except the blood of the Canaanites or other enemies). Like the murderer, any person "devoted" by a vow to Yahweh must surely be put to death (Lev. 27:28-29).

That Yahweh Himself often executes the death penalty has been shown already by citing several examples of His punishments, and the same thing is indicated, again and again, in the priestly statutes. Any serious infringement of the ceremonial rules designed to preserve the holiness of Yahweh's worship costs a man his life (cf. Num. 1:51, 53; 3:10, 38; 18:22). It is small wonder that with such an all-powerful and destructive God in their midst the people complain to Moses: "Behold, we perish, we are undone, we are all undone. Every one that cometh near, that cometh near unto the tabernacle of Jehovah, dieth: shall we perish all of us?" (Num. 17:12-13) Though the Levites have special privileges of nearness, it is fatal for them to go too far and encroach upon the sacred prerogatives of the priests (Num. 4:15, 17-20; 18:3, 7).

The proposed war over the altar erected by the East-Jordan tribes is apparently motivated less by intertribal jealousy than by fear of Yahweh's wrath (cf. Josh. 22:12, 17-18, 20). When Reuben and Gad and Manasseh explain their action, and vigorously disavow any intention to offer sacrifice upon this new altar or to rebel in any way against Yahweh, Phinehas the priest tells them with great relief: "This day we know that Jehovah is in the midst of us, because ye have not committed this trespass against Jehovah: now have ye delivered the children of Israel out of the hand of Jehovah" (Josh. 22:31).

Though the Israelites frequently experience Yahweh's wrath, He purposes to be their God, and among the nations He is definitely on their side—or, more accurately, He demonstrates His own power and holiness by overwhelming their enemies.

Yahweh hardens Pharaoh's heart so as to give occasion for showing His power through the plagues (cf. Ex. 7:3-5 and Ex. 7:19-20*a*; 8:5-6; 8:16-17, 19; 9:8-9; 12:12-13). The slaying of the Egyptian first-born is later recalled with zest (Num. 33: 3-4). When Yahweh smites the Egyptians' first-born, He hallows for Himself the first-born of the Israelites, and later when the Levites are ordained for His service they are regarded as substitutes for these hallowed first-born (Num. 3:12-13; 8:17-18). After the Israelites' escape, Yahweh again hardens Pharaoh's heart, this time to instigate pursuit, so as to "get honor" by drowning the Egyptian hosts (Ex. 14:4, 8-9, 15, 16b-18, 21-23, 26-27a, 28a, 29).

Yahweh is determined to execute vengeance upon Midian, and to accomplish this the Israelites under Moses slay every male among the Midianites, burn their cities, and take their unmarried women captive (Num. 31:1-18). Gad and Reuben must "go before Yahweh" to the war across the Jordan (Num. 32:20-23). Finally, in all, "about forty thousand ready armed for war passed over before Jehovah unto battle, to the plains of Jericho" (Josh. 4:13).

With regard to the nations inhabiting Canaan, Yahweh's command is to drive them all out, destroy all their images and sanctuaries, and assign their land to the tribes of Israel by lot (Num. 33:51-56). On account of their ill-advised covenant with them, the Israelites cannot slay the Gibeonites, so they decide to make them "hewers of wood and drawers of water" (Josh. 9:20-21).

In giving directions for the making and use of the silver trumpets, Yahweh promises His aid in war. "And when ye go to war in your land against the adversary that oppresseth you, then ye shall sound an alarm with the trumpets; and ye shall be remembered before Jehovah your God, and ye shall be saved from your enemies" (Num. 10:9).

It is perhaps worth noting that both in the first census (Num. 1:2-3) and in the second census (Num. 26:2) only the men of war are counted.

It seems relevant also to notice the attitude of this document toward marriage with other peoples. Esau's Hittite wives are "a grief of mind unto Isaac and Rebekah" (Gen. 26:34-35), and the parents take good care to insure Jacob's marriage to one of their own relatives (Gen. 27:46; 28:1-2). During the period of the wanderings, an Israelite who marries a Midianitish woman is killed to avert a plague (Num. 25:6-18). Women from other nations are, of course, thought of as endangering the religious integrity of the people of Yahweh.

The God of the priestly document is a distant being, approachable by His people only through specially commissioned mediators. His requirements are predominantly cultic, and any infringement of them is likely to be fatal. His supremacy in the universe is complete and is wielded without apparent effort; but though He is the Creator and Ruler of all mankind, He dwells with only one people. For this people, if they obey Him, He may be expected to respond to the priestly invocation:

> Jehovah bless thee, and keep thee:
> Jehovah make his face to shine upon thee, and be gracious unto thee:
> Jehovah lift up his countenance upon thee, and give thee peace (Num. 6:24-26).

FURTHER PROPHETIC WORK

OBADIAH

In this brief "vision" of triumphant revenge upon Edom, almost every word has a bearing upon our study. Edom was being reduced to sore straits by invading Arabians,[6] and naturally many of the Jews believed this to be Yahweh's way of paying off an old score, and requiting the Edomites for taking sides with the enemy and plundering Jerusalem after its capture by the Babylonians. They have given the unfortunate Jews taunts instead of sympathy; now they will receive their just deserts, and it is time for the Jews to taunt them.

Obadiah is the spokesman for these vengefully exultant Jews. He sees in the events of his own day the fulfillment of an older oracle, which represented Yahweh as summoning the nations to battle for the overthrow of Edom (vss. 1-4, 8-9).

It is easy to find a motive for Yahweh's vengeance upon Edom; the God of Jacob shares His people's hatred and desire for

[6] Cf. Bewer, *International Critical Commentary* on *Obadiah*, pp. 10-11.

retaliation for the brutal unbrotherliness of Esau (vss. 10-12). Now, "as thou hast done, it shall be done unto thee; thy dealings shall return upon thine own head (vs. 15b).

In the two appendices, vss. 15a, 16-18, and vss. 19-21, a later writer or writers made Edom's disaster the most welcome feature of an imminent day of divine judgment and retaliation upon all the nations. Not content with the demolition of Edom, Yahweh's people shall push out in all directions, to conquer and to possess the territory of their neighbors. Then at last, with Israel triumphant and the others subjugated, the kingdom shall be Yahweh's! (vs. 21b)

The Yahweh of Obadiah thus appears to be a national God, powerful enough to avenge His people most terribly upon their enemies. In the appendices, His reign, to follow His "day" of reckoning, has no evident ethical connotation, but signifies merely the triumphant realization of the ambitions of a militaristic, revengeful, self-satisfied nationalism.

ISAIAH 15-16

No prophecy of doom upon a neighboring nation is more remarkable in spirit than the oracle concerning Moab, in Isaiah 15-16, coming from the same period as Obadiah's song of hate against Edom.

The writer's heart "crieth out for Moab" (15:5a) as he witnesses the destruction that the invading Arabs are bringing upon city after city—"my heart soundeth like a harp for Moab, and mine inward parts for Kir-heres" (16:11). He beseeches his countrymen to "hide the outcasts; betray not the fugitive" (16:3).

This prophet has little to say about Yahweh's part in all this, but, in his demonstration of a human sympathy that leaps over national boundaries, we feel a spirit akin to that of the one who just a little later related the story of Ruth the Moabitess.

MALACHI

After the Temple had been rebuilt and the cult resumed, no signal material prosperity, such as Haggai had anticipated, came to the Jewish community. Hard times and discouragement gradually led to laxness in regard to the cult on the part of both priests and people, a weakening faith in Yahweh's care for them and even in His justice, and a growing tendency to mingle freely with the peoples round about them and intermarry with them. In this situation, a prophet (called "Malachi" from the Hebrew "my messenger" in 3:1) arose to show his people the error of their ways and what he believed to be the true nature of their God.

The attitude toward other nations exhibited by the Yahweh of Malachi is striking.

The prophet's argument to prove Yahweh's love for Israel is—His inveterate ruthless partisanship! "Yet ye say, Wherein hast thou loved us? Was not Esau Jacob's brother? saith Jehovah: yet I loved Jacob; but Esau I hated, and made his mountains a desolation . . ." (1: 2b-3; cf. 1: 4-5).

It surely seems as though a different conception is being offered us when Malachi begins another argument: "Have we not all one father? Hath not one God created us?" (2:10a) but the illusion soon passes, for we discover that "we" who are thus "brothers" are only the Jews. Only they belong to Yahweh; a woman from another nation is "the daughter of a foreign god" (2:11b). To marry such a woman is to profane "the holiness [or "sanctuary"] of Jehovah which he loveth" (2:11) and Yahweh will cut off a man who does this, and all his descendants (2:12).

In the heat of a denunciation of the Jews' defilement of His cult, Malachi represents Yahweh as saying: "For from the rising of the sun even unto the going down of the same my name shall be [better, "is"] great among the Gentiles; and in every place incense shall be [is] offered unto my name, and a pure offering: for my name shall be [is] great among the Gentiles, saith Jehovah of hosts" (1:11; cf. 1:14b). The idea seems to be that "the heathen bring all their sacrifices to Yahweh, since He is the sole reality behind all the gods that are worshipped, and their sacrifices are purer and more acceptable than those of the Jews."[7] In view, however, of Yahweh's "hatred" of Edom and

[7] Bewer, *The Literature of the Old Testament*, p. 255. For a discussion of other possible interpretations, see footnote on that page, and also Smith, J. M. P., *International Critical Commentary* on *Malachi*, pp. 30-33.

the limitation of His concern to the Jews in 2:10-11, we can hardly say that this generous estimate of the heathen, introduced to throw Israel's sin into sharper relief, indicates any significant relation between Yahweh and other nations.

After the hoped-for repentance and reformation of the Jews, and their resultant material blessings from Yahweh, "all nations" shall be spectators, to call them happy, but there is no evidence that others will share in the blessing (3:12).

Toward His own people, Yahweh is represented as justly indignant. A father, or a master, or an earthly governor, would be shown much greater honor and fear and consideration than they have given to their God (1:6, 8), with their half-hearted offerings of polluted bread and sick, blemished animals (1:7-8, 12-14). The priests have corrupted the covenant "of life and peace" which Yahweh made with Levi (2:1-8).

The ethical sins for which Yahweh will judge the people are mentioned (3:5), but, on the whole, the greater stress is on cultic sins, and if only they will "bring the whole tithe into the storehouse, that there may be food in my house," Yahweh of hosts will "open the windows of heaven" and pour out an overwhelming blessing (3:10).

The way to repentance is definitely open (3:7b). It is expected that some, at least, will return to Yahweh in reverent fear, and He will spare these righteous ones (3:17-18). Alas for the wicked then! Yahweh will utterly consume them in His approaching "day," and part of the joy of the righteous will be to tread them down (4:1-3).

According to the later addition, 4:4-6,[8] Yahweh will send Elijah before the "great and terrible day of Jehovah" to improve conditions, "lest I come and smite the earth with a curse" [a ban devoting everything to destruction].

On the whole, Malachi's Yahweh of hosts is a God of just one people, greatly concerned to keep them separate from others and to have them evince loyalty to Him through a revived devotion to His cult. He will be seen eventually to punish the wicked with

[8] Cf. Smith, J. M. P., *International Critical Commentary* on *Malachi*, pp. 81-83.

terrific destruction, but meanwhile His people have an opportunity to reform their ways and be restored to His favor.

MEMOIRS OF NEHEMIAH AND OF EZRA

The books of Ezra and Nehemiah in their present form quite clearly come from the author of Chronicles, and his contributions to them will be included in the discussion of his larger work. The Chronicler's account of events in the early post-exilic period is based, however, upon earlier documents of much greater historical value—memoirs of Nehemiah, evidently written shortly after the close of his governorship in 432 B.C.,[9] and of Ezra "the priest, the scribe," probably written a little later. These two men, conscious of the favor and guidance of their God, worked to restore Yahweh's people to a sense of their religious uniqueness and national dignity—Nehemiah through his brave and enthusiastic leadership in rebuilding the city wall, Ezra through introducing and teaching the Priest Code and inspiring a new loyalty to Yahweh's written statutes, and both Nehemiah and Ezra through a persistent effort for racial purity and exclusiveness.

In Nehemiah's memoirs, "Jehovah, the God of heaven, the great and terrible God, that keepeth covenant and lovingkindness with them that love him and keep his commandments" (1:5) is graciously directing and shielding those engaged in an enterprise which carries out His will (2:8, 18, 20; 4:15; 6:16; 7:5). He is close to His people, capable of hearing and responding to prayer offered anywhere, whenever Nehemiah feels special need of His help (2:4; 4:9).

God may be expected to continue His favor to His people, and to reward special faithfulness. Nehemiah several times appeals: "Remember unto me, O my God, for good, all that I have done for this people" (5:19; cf. 13:14, 22, 31). God may also be counted upon to punish the wicked, as indicated in Nehemiah's imprecations against the enemies who are taunting the Jews and trying to hinder their work (4:4, 5; 6:14) and later

[9] Cf. Bewer, *The Literature of the Old Testament*, p. 280.

against those Jews who have "defiled the priesthood" by mixed marriages (13:29).

Since enemies were planning to attack and slay the Jews during their work on the wall, the Jews worked "with their swords, their spears, and their bows" in hand (4:13, 16-17), ready to fight at any moment in self-defense, and trusting that "our God will fight for us" (4:20).

Nehemiah is convinced that he is pleasing God by casting Tobiah the Ammonite out of the Temple (13:4-8), and cursing and punishing those who "trespass against our God in marrying foreign women," making these men swear not to permit the intermarriage of the children with foreigners (13:23-29).

According to Ezra, "Jehovah the God of our fathers" (Ez. 7:27; 10:11), "Jehovah my (our) God" (7:28; 9:6, 8), or "the God of Israel" (8:35; 9:4, 15), is the Creator and Preserver of heaven and earth (Neh. 9:6).[10] This omnipotent Yahweh helps His own favored ones by influence upon the attitude of the Persian king (Ez. 7:27-28; 9:9), by strength to undertake a great project (7:28b), and by adequate protection from any dangers on the way back to Jerusalem (8:21-23, 31).

Yahweh is also a righteous God, punishing iniquity but showing mercy to those who repent and reform. This merciful attitude has been shown throughout the history of the nation (Neh. 9:7-31), and will be seen in the present generation if the people do their part (Ez. 9:5-10:4). Their terrible sin is intermarriage with their heathen neighbors, "so that the holy seed have mingled themselves with the peoples of the lands" (Ez. 9:1-2). The land is unclean in Yahweh's eyes through the abominations of these peoples, and His command has been not to allow intermarriage nor to "seek their peace or their prosperity for ever; that ye may be strong" (Ez. 9:12). The way to turn away the "fierce wrath of our God" and to regain His favor is to confess this sin and put away all the foreign wives (Ez. 10:10-19).

In these writings, then, the God of heaven is the righteous but merciful God of the Jews alone, opposing any who interfere

[10] Nehemiah 8-10 should be included in the memoirs of Ezra (cf. Bewer, op. cit., p. 282), though an editor has rewritten them in the third person.

with them and wanting them to shun all relationship with other peoples, in order that they may completely serve Him.

ARAMAIC DOCUMENT IN EZRA 4:8 TO 6:18

Another of the Chronicler's sources was an Aramaic document now preserved in Ezra 4:8 to 6:18, composed mainly of letters between the Persian king and his officials regarding the rebuilding of the Temple and the walls of Jerusalem.

As in the writings just discussed, the God of the Jews is "the great God" (Ez. 5:8), and the "God of heaven (and earth)" (5:11, 12; 6:9, 10). His care and protection are for the Jews, who are doing His will (5:5). The opponents of the Jews are finally proved to be in the wrong, and are required not only to stop troubling them, but to give them help toward the expense of building (Ez. 6:6-8), and Darius includes in his letter a curse upon any future enemies of the Temple (6:11-12).

RUTH

Out of the period when Ezra and Nehemiah were seeking the religious good of the Jewish people through the enforcement of a rigid exclusiveness, annulling "mixed marriages" already contracted with women from neighboring peoples and trying to imbue the Jews with a thorough-going intolerance of all foreigners, there rose a voice of protest. Instead of thundering a denunciation of the exclusive policy that seemed to be gaining headway, this writer told a simple story, so beautiful and appealing that its spirit of tolerance would steal into the consciousness of many who would not have listened to a broadside harangue.

To be sure, the thought of the writer still moves within the limits of henotheism. Yahweh is the God of Israel, and not the God of the Moabites, which god, in turn, has his own distinct identity and is worshipped by his own people.

Naomi "had heard in the country of Moab how that Jehovah had visited his people in giving them bread" (1:6). When Ruth proves unwilling to leave her mother-in-law, Naomi urges: "Behold, thy sister-in-law is gone back unto her people, and unto her god: return thou after thy sister-in-law" (1:15). Unshaken in her decision to cling to Naomi, Ruth protests that she will share all phases of Naomi's life, including: "Thy people shall be my people, and thy God my God" (1:16d). Later in the story, Boaz invokes upon Ruth a "full reward" from "Jehovah, the God of Israel, under whose wings thou art come to take refuge" (2:12).

Moreover, we may note in passing that the book of Ruth presents no new idea of the nature of Yahweh's relation to people. As in the usual thought of the Old Testament, He is the direct cause of misfortune or sorrow. Though no reason is indicated for Yahweh's punishing her, Naomi interprets the death of her husband and sons as a special act of Yahweh against her (1:13b, 20-21). Good fortune as well as ill is apparently traced to direct divine action (4:13).

This book gives, then, no new interpretation of Yahweh's nature or character, nor does it blur at all the distinction between different nationalities. Its uniqueness, which gives it significance for the present study, lies in its consistent assumption of easy, natural, friendly relationships between nationals of neighboring countries, and in its exquisite portrayal of human worth and personal charm and virtue in characters who to Jews were "foreigners."

Moab is the place of refuge for the famine-stricken Judahite family (1:1). When Mahlon and Chilion marry Moabitish women, it seems neither unnatural nor undesirable (1:4).

The character of both of these women is attractively painted. Naomi testifies of them both that they have dealt kindly with the dead and with her (1:8). Both call forth from her a heartfelt prayer for blessing from Yahweh (1:8-9). Both indicate deep affection for her, weep at the thought of separation, and offer to go with her unto her people (1:9-10).

As a further evidence of the writer's tolerant attitude toward "mixed marriages," when Boaz announces to the elders and the people in the gate: "Moreover Ruth the Moabitess, the wife of Mahlon, have I purchased to be my wife . . .: ye are witnesses this day" (4:10), instead of being shocked at the marriage of this prominent man with a foreigner, they all invoke Yahweh's blessing upon the marriage (2:11-12). The climax of the story is the birth of a son to Boaz and Ruth: "he is the father of Jesse, the father of David" (4:17). Ruth the Moabitess is an ancestress of David!

The most telling aspect of the story is the writer's portrayal of Ruth as one of the most winsome characters in literature. Her utter devotion to Naomi leads her to break all the ties that bind her to her own people and her religion, forfeiting, as it might seem, her hope of another marriage—in complete abandonment to her purpose of sharing the experience of her bereaved mother-in-law (1:16-17). After their arrival in Beth-lehem, Ruth is eager to labor to support Naomi and herself (2:2); she is always cheerfully obedient to Naomi's directions (3:5) and considerate of her (2:14b, 18b). So unusual is her loyal devotion that it has evidently been a matter of common talk among the people, for Boaz has heard all about it (2:11; 3:11b). At the close of the story, the women of the village pay their tribute to Ruth, "thy daughter-in-law, who loveth thee, who is better to thee than seven sons" (4:15).

The picture is not one-sided in its appreciation of Ruth, the foreigner. She stands among Jewish characters of nobility and charm—Boaz, with his cordial recognition of Ruth's great kindness to Naomi, and his constant gallantry and unlimited generosity toward Ruth; Naomi herself, a character whose fairness and thoughtful consideration for Ruth and Orpah and whose devoted effort for Ruth's welfare after the return to Judah indicate a strength and lovableness well fitted to call forth such an affectionate loyalty as Ruth's.

However, attractive as are all the chief characters in this story, the author is careful to keep us mindful of the fact that his heroine is a foreigner. Though she has been fully introduced in the opening verses, and the reader is not likely to forget that she has come from Moab, again and again she is referred to as "Ruth the Moabitess" (1:22; 2:2, 21; 4:5, 10; cf. 2:6). Ruth's amazed response to the special kindness of Boaz is: "Why have I found favor in thy sight, that thou shouldest take knowledge of me, seeing I am a foreigner?" (2:10; cf. 2:13)

A foreigner, then, a Moabitess, one of a nationality that the Deuteronomists had barred forever from the assembly of Yahweh (Deut. 23:3), is here a model of virtue and grace, is the wife in turn of two Israelites of honorable standing in the community, is admired and praised by all who know her, and apparently is specially favored by Yahweh Himself, since He grants her the highest conceivable blessing by making her an ancestress of the great King David. This writer's attitude toward foreigners would take from henotheism most of its usual connotation with regard to war.

CHAPTER VII

PROPHECY AND NARRATIVE FROM THE LATE PERSIAN AND EARLY GREEK PERIODS

1. Joel and Other Prophetic Fragments—2. Esther—3. Chronicles—4. Jonah

JOEL AND OTHER PROPHETIC FRAGMENTS

JOEL

At some time not clearly indicated, perhaps late in the fifth or early in the fourth century B.C.,[1] a locust plague of unprecedented severity occasioned the utterances of the prophet Joel. Whether his thought leaped further to the conception of the day of Yahweh's judgment upon the nations is not certain, but it is quite conceivable that the nucleus of this part of the book also comes from Joel.

In the former sections of Joel's work, Yahweh is a God who smites His people with a mighty, resistless army of locusts (2: 5, 7) and with drought, so that they have no grain nor fruit nor wine, and, worst of all, "the meal-offering and the drink-offering are cut off from the house of Jehovah" (1:9a). Apparently the cult is of supreme importance to Yahweh—and yet the calamity which interrupts it must have been brought on by Him! Certainly there is urgent need for placating Him and procuring a cessation of His punishment (1:13-14, 19).

The traditional conception of Yahweh offers in this crisis two grounds for hope that He may relent and restore Judah to material prosperity. In the first place, He is a merciful God, responding to His people when they turn sincerely to Him, rending their hearts and not their garments (2:12-14). Secondly, He is a God jealous for His prestige in the eyes of other nations,

---

[1] Cf. Bewer, *The Literature of the Old Testament*, p. 395.

and hence not likely to permit His "heritage" to be long an object of reproach and derision (2: 17-19, 26).

The other main section of the book, dealing with the latter days, has in view sometimes only Judah and sometimes all the nations.

Apparently, only "all flesh" among the Jews [2] will experience the ecstatic states resulting from the outpouring of Yahweh's Spirit (2: 28-29), while clearly only Jews are contemplated in the promise of the remnant in Zion (2: 32).

The dominant feature of the coming day, however, is the participation of all the nations in its fierce warfare and tumult, and in disastrous judgment from Yahweh. "Proclaim ye this among the nations; prepare war; stir up the mighty men; let all the men of war draw near, let them come up. Beat your plowshares into swords, and your pruning-hooks into spears: let the weak say, I am strong" (3: 9-10; cf. vss. 11-13).

The editor of the book stresses Israel's safety amid this almost universal destruction; Yahweh "will be a refuge unto his people," will dwell with them in Zion, and make the city "holy," with no strangers passing through it (3: 16b-17).

In harmony with this idea, another passage from the editor (3: 18-21) portrays the marvelous future prosperity of Judah against the background of the desolation of her hostile neighbors. Yahweh will fully avenge the blood of His people. Similarly, according to the interpolation in 3: 2b-8, Yahweh will do to Tyre and Sidon and Philistia with vengeful zest the very same injuries which they have done to Judah!

The Yahweh of the book of Joel is thus a God of might and vengeance, responsive to penitent appeal from His own people, but apparently relentless toward the other nations.

ISAIAH 19: 1-15 AND 23: 1-14

These passages, predicting the downfall of Egypt and of Sidon, perhaps at the hand of Artaxerxes Ochus about the middle of the fourth century, bear on our problem because Yahweh is represented as riding upon a swift cloud to bring civil war and destruction upon Egypt, and to give it over "into the hand of a

[2] Cf. Bewer, *International Critical Commentary* on *Joel*, p. 123.

cruel lord" (19:1-4), whereas Sidon meets her humiliating fate because "Jehovah of hosts hath purposed it, to stain the pride of all glory, to bring into contempt all the honorable of the earth" (23:9).

The conception that nothing can happen among nations except as the result of Yahweh's purpose makes Him responsible for a vast amount of brutality.

An appendix to the latter oracle anticipates a time when the profits of Tyre's trading shall be "holiness to Jehovah"— because these riches will be in the hands of the Jews, not because Tyre will know Yahweh (23:18).[3]

ISAIAH 24-27

The apocalypse in Isaiah 24-27 probably comes from the time of Alexander's conquests.[4] It portrays Yahweh as exercising His punitive might against "the host of the high ones" and "the kings of the earth" (24:21), devastating strong cities (25:2), treading down Moab (25:10-12), devouring His adversaries with fire (26:11; cf. vs. 14), and slaying leviathan with "his hard and great and strong sword" (27:1).

Besides this aspect of terrible power, however, which has many parallels in other writings, we have here in one passage the noteworthy conception that Yahweh of hosts will make a feast in His holy mountain "unto all peoples" (25:6), not the bloody sacrificial feast that we have sometimes found accompanying some great slaughter by Yahweh, but a feast representing beneficence and mercy to all peoples. "And he will destroy in this mountain the face of the covering that covereth all peoples, and the veil that is spread over all nations. He hath swallowed up death for ever; and the Lord Jehovah will wipe away tears from off all faces" (25:7-8).

GENESIS 14

Practically the only war story in Genesis (cf., however, Gen. 34) comes from this late period, and recounts how Abram, with his three hundred and eighteen "trained men, born in his house" rescued his nephew Lot by defeating the kings who in battle had captured him and his fellow-citizens of Sodom. The reason

[3] Cf. Bewer, *The Literature of the Old Testament*, p. 398.
[4] Cf. Bewer, *op. cit.*, p. 399.

for Abram's victory is the fact that "God Most High, possessor of heaven and earth," delivered his enemies into his hand (14: 19-20).

ISAIAH 19: 18-25

Of all the Old Testament writings, none is more deeply significant for this study than a brief anonymous passage found in Isaiah 19: 18-25. Influenced, perhaps, by the closer contacts with other cultures made possible during the Greek period, a prophet here ventures to envisage a time when Yahweh will not be the God of Israel alone, but when "the Egyptians shall know Jehovah," and worship Him with sacrifice and oblation and vows, when "Jehovah will smite Egypt, smiting and healing; and they shall return unto Jehovah, and he will be entreated of them, and will heal them" (19: 21-22).

But more than this—a day will come when the inveterate rivalry between the two great empires of antiquity will be done away with, when "there shall be a highway out of Egypt to Assyria" and friendly intercourse, even fellowship in worship, will take the place of the campaigns of armies—"'and the Assyrian shall come into Egypt, and the Egyptian into Assyria; and the Egyptians shall worship with the Assyrians" (19: 23).

What will be Israel's place in such a day? We might expect that if Israel's God is to be universally worshipped Israel will have a place of preëminence. So would most prophets have said—but no, Israel will be just a nation among nations, "the third with Egypt and with Assyria, a blessing in the midst of the earth," not even possessing any unique claim upon Yahweh, "for that Jehovah of hosts hath blessed them, saying, Blessed be Egypt my people, and Assyria the work of my hands, and Israel mine inheritance" (19: 24-25).

Israel's ultimate vocation, then, is to be a nation bringing blessing to other peoples, in a day when they, too, worship Yahweh and are as close to Him as Israel herself. Though he does not deal with the method of its attainment, this prophet dares to believe that somehow the hope of Deutero-Isaiah for universal salvation through Israel's ministry will eventually be realized, and, further, that international friendship will one day replace war.

Esther

The book of Esther comes probably from the period soon after the collapse of the Persian empire. A writer familiar with conditions of life under the Persian kings chose that time for the plot of his story depicting the relations of the Jews in the East with the peoples among whom they dwelt, and explaining the origin of the Feast of Purim. Since the book does not mention the name of God, it may not be strictly relevant to discuss it here. However, the intensely nationalistic spirit of this "historical romance" makes it significant material for any investigation dealing with attitudes toward war.

The assumption throughout is that the Jews are the innocent victims of Haman's villainous plotting. Haman's only provocation is the fact that "Mordecai bowed not down, nor did him reverence" (3:2b) when the king had expressly commanded everyone to do so, and of course this persistent refusal was justified, since "he was a Jew" (3:4b). The author's studied avoidance of any reference to the deity prevents a fuller explanation of why a Jew could not do such homage to a man, but this would not be needed by his Jewish audience. Haman's desire for revenge embraces all the Jews in the kingdom of Ahasuerus (3:6). When he seeks the king's permission to destroy them, he characterizes them as a people scattered throughout the kingdom, whose "laws are diverse from those of every people; neither keep they the king's laws; therefore it is not for the king's profit to suffer them" (3:8). The Jews would have admitted, with pride, their unique laws and their disobedience to any laws contrary to theirs. The point of view determines whether this is a divinely bestowed distinction or a crime against the welfare of the empire.

The command is finally given "to destroy, to slay, and to cause to perish, all Jews, both young and old, little children and women, in one day . . . and to take the spoil of them for a prey" (3:13). It sounds strangely like some of Yahweh's commands to His people with regard to the Canaanites during the conquest period—but such a comparison suggests a possible equality of human worth which would be utterly foreign to the conception of either writing.

Though the author will not speak of Yahweh, it seems as though the "great mourning among the Jews" when the decree is published (4:3) must indicate an effort to prevail upon their national God to arise in their behalf. A similar possibility of rescue through Yahweh seems to underlie Mordecai's veiled message to Esther, asserting that if she fails to do her part "then will relief and deliverance arise to the Jews from another place" (4:13-14). What, too, but Yahweh's help can be the object of the fasting of the Jews for Esther before she goes into the presence of the king on her dangerous errand? (4:16)

A belief in some strange power either in the Jews or protecting them seems to be implied in the remark of the wise men and Zeresh to Haman: "If Mordecai, before whom thou hast begun to fall, be of the seed of the Jews, thou shalt not prevail against him, but shalt surely fall before him" (7:13).

After the wicked Haman has been dramatically exposed, and hanged on the very gallows that he had built for Mordecai, and after Mordecai and Esther have been exalted to all the authority that Haman had formerly held, comes the part of the story most important for this study.

By Mordecai's decree in the name of the king, the Jews are permitted to defend themselves, and to do to their enemies exactly what had formerly been contemplated against the Jews, "to destroy, to slay, and to cause to perish, all the power of the people and province that would assault them, their little ones and women, and to take the spoil of them for a prey" (8:11). After the publication of this order, "the Jews had light and gladness, and joy and honor" (8:16).

In introducing the events of the thirteenth of Adar, the author reminds us again with the greatest apparent satisfaction that this is "the day that the enemies of the Jews hoped to have rule over them, whereas it was turned to the contrary, that the Jews had rule over them that hated them" (9:1b). On that day, "the Jews smote all their enemies with the stroke of the sword, and with slaughter and destruction, and did what they would unto them that hated them. And in Shushan the palace the Jews slew and destroyed five hundred men" (9:5-6). Happy day! However, the Jews' appetite for bloody revenge had only been whetted by the day's good work, and upon Esther's request to the king they are permitted to continue their slaughter in Shushan the next day (9:15-16). The days following their triumph become days of feasting and gladness (9:17-19), to be observed yearly "as the days wherein the Jews had rest from their enemies" (9:20-22).

The concluding picture of Mordecai is of one "next unto king Ahasuerus, and great among the Jews, and accepted of the multitude of his brethren, seeking the good of his people, and speaking peace to all his seed" (10:3). One wonders what this benevolent loyalty to his own people involved for the other subjects of King Ahasuerus during the rest of Mordecai's régime.

The book of Esther, then, has as its heroine a woman of beauty and courage, combined with a loyalty to the Jews which prompts her at one time to risk her life in interceding for her imperiled people and at another to request another day of bloodthirsty vengeance for her triumphant people. As its hero, the book has a stubbornly loyal Jew, alert to everything that affects his people, sure of their ultimate triumph, and insatiable in his ambition for them, once the tables have been turned in their favor.

May we not go further and characterize the unmentioned Yahweh of this writing? After the sackcloth and the fasting there comes with unerring precision event after event in the dramatic plot that culminates in such bloody victory. Has not a Power responded to the fasting and come to the aid of His own people as in the stories of the days of old? In this story where human life as such counts for nothing, but the life of the Jews must be protected at all costs, the outcome could certainly not have been different if a national warrior-god had come full-armed to the defense of His people.

CHRONICLES

The writer who, about 300 B.C., surveyed the history of the united kingdom and of Judah in Chronicles, Ezra, and Nehemiah, had as his sources our books of Samuel and Kings, the memoirs of Ezra and Nehemiah, and various other less reliable documents.

Writings from Late Persian and Early Greek Periods 129

His selection and presentation of material drawn from these sources is guided by a philosophy of history in which two ideas are dominant—complete divine retributive justice, and the supreme importance of the Temple and its services. The latter conception leads to an idealization of David and Solomon, who made the Temple possible, and to the neglect of the history of the schismatic northern kingdom, which had, of course, been absorbed into the Assyrian Empire about four centuries before this writer's time.

God's reward for men pleasing to Him is a frequent theme (e.g., I Chr. 11:9; 12:18; 14:2; 17:8-13; II Chr. 1:1, 12; 26:5; 27:6). David's words to Solomon, "If thou seek him, he will be found of thee; but if thou forsake him, he will cast thee off for ever" (I Chr. 28:9b; cf. II Chr. 7:11-22; 15:1-2; 30:8-9) are illustrated by every part of the story.

The divine punishment of the wicked is seen in such cases as Yahweh's slaying Saul for trespassing against Him (I Chr. 10:13-14) [5] or His smiting Uzzah with instantaneous death (I Chr. 13:9-10; retained from II Sam. 6:6-7), or smiting King Uzziah with leprosy for encroaching upon the prerogative of the priest by offering incense. As in II Sam. 24:12-13, David's census necessitates punishment by Yahweh with either famine, or the sword of enemies, or pestilence, "the sword of Jehovah" (I Chr. 21:11-12). The Chronicler's theology, however, was offended by the idea that Yahweh Himself moved David to take the impious census, so here it is done at the instigation of "Satan" (I Chr. 21:1).[6] Nevertheless, he apparently adopts without protest the idea, voiced by Micaiah, that Yahweh sends a lying spirit into the prophets, to entice Ahab to death at Ramoth-Gilead (II Chr. 18:19-22). Any measures seem to be justified against the sinful Ahab and his house; Jehu is referred to as the one "whom Jehovah had anointed to cut off the house of Ahab" (II Chr. 22:7), and Jehoshaphat is sternly reprimanded for allying himself with Ahab: "Shouldest thou help the wicked, and love them that hate Jehovah? for this

[5] In I Samuel 13:13, 14 and 15:23, Yahweh "rejects Saul from being king," but He is not said to have slain him.

[6] The old idea of the sinfulness of the census is not a little incongruous in this writing, filled as it is with census statistics.

thing wrath is upon thee from before Jehovah" (II Chr. 19:2). There is no hope for such as Ahab!

The unique relation between Yahweh and His chosen people, Israel, is often expressed. In David's psalm of thanksgiving when the ark is brought to Jerusalem, made up of fragments taken from various parts of the Psalter, all the earth is to tremble before Yahweh, recognize the fact of His reign, or even worship Him (I Chr. 16:29-31), but other passages in the same psalm make it clear that this conveys no thought of any possible intimacy between Yahweh and other nations, but is just the result of overflowing jubilation at the lovingkindness of "Jehovah, the God of Israel" (16:36) toward His "chosen ones" (16:13), His "anointed ones" (16:22). There is no question as to Yahweh's universal control (e.g., I Chr. 17:20; 20:11-12; Ez. 1:2), but along with it is always the idea expressed by David in one of his prayers: "For thy people Israel didst thou make thine own people forever; and thou, Jehovah, becamest their God" (I Chr. 17:22; cf. 17:21, 24; II Chr. 2:12). At the time of Solomon's accession we find the interesting notice: "Then Solomon sat on the throne of Jehovah as king instead of David his father" (I Chr. 29:23). After the return of the Jews under Zerubbabel, when their neighbors offer to help build the Temple, "for we seek your God, as ye do," they are rebuffed with the answer: "Ye have nothing to do with us in building a house unto our God; but we ourselves together will build unto Jehovah, the God of Israel . . ." (Ez. 4:2-3).

Yahweh's great concern is to have this chosen people worship Him alone, and do it in just the place and just the manner prescribed. To abolish the high places or reform the ritual is the greatest glory of any king. So important was every detail of the architecture and furnishing of the Temple that the "pattern" of it had been revealed to David "in writing from the hand of Jehovah" (I Chr. 28:19).

God's help in battle figures prominently in Chronicles. For instance, during one of their wars the trans-Jordanic tribes were divinely aided against the Hagrites, "for they cried to God in the battle . . . there fell many slain, because the war was of God" (I Chr. 5:20, 22; cf. 11:14; 12:22; 14:11, 15-17). In the list of David's victories over the neighboring nations (I Chr. 18:1-13), stressing the great number slain and the reduction of these nations to vassalage, we have the refrain, "And Jehovah gave victory to David, whithersoever he went" (18:6b, 13b). Abijah's exhortation to Jeroboam and the Israelites not to fight against the divinely ordained dynasty of David, supported by the divinely ordained priests and Levites, closes, "And, behold, God is with us at our head, . . . O children of Israel, fight ye not against Jehovah, the God of your fathers" (II Chr. 13: 4-20; cf. 14:11-15; 16:7-9; 19:31b; 26:6-8). Jehoshaphat's prayer for help in battle brings the response: "Fear not ye . . . for the battle is not yours, but God's"; his army moves out with the Levitical singers leading, praising Yahweh for His lovingkindness, and as soon as they begin to sing, Yahweh causes the allied enemy armies to destroy one another (II Chr. 20:1-30; cf. 32:7-8, 21).

In the genealogical tables and the census lists, we find great emphasis on "mighty men of valor," men "able to go forth to war," and so on (I Chr. 7:5, 9, 11, 40; 8:40; 12:23-38; 26: 30, 32; II Chr. 17:13-18; 25:5; 26:11-15). Sometimes the qualifications of the valiant warriors are given in more elaborate detail (I Chr. 5:18; 11:11, 20, 22-23; 12:1-3, 8, 14).

When His people need to be punished, the God of Israel as a rule instigates some foreign nation to war against them (I Chr. 5:25-26; 9:1b; II Chr. 12:2; 21:10, 16-17; 24:24; 28:5-6, 16-23; 33:11; 36:17).

Peace is an occasional gift from Yahweh (e.g., II Chr. 14:6; 15:15b). He gives rest from enemies by enabling a favored king to hold them all in subjection (I Chr. 22:9, 18) or sometimes by making the fear, or terror, of Yahweh fall upon all the neighboring kingdoms (II Chr. 17:10; 20:29-30).

The reason why David should not build the Temple is: "Thou hast shed blood abundantly, and hast made great wars: thou shalt not build a house unto my name, because thou hast shed much blood upon the earth in my sight" (I Chr. 22:8-10; cf. 28:3). In Kings, the impression is that David was too busy fighting to devote himself to the project of building the Temple— in Chronicles, his having shed much blood in war unfits him for such a task as building Yahweh's house. This is a unique idea— that bloodshed is any religious disadvantage in Yahweh's sight. However, we must not stress it too much, in view of Yahweh's own participation in war throughout Chronicles, and the fact that, apparently with Yahweh's favor, "out of the spoil won in battles did they dedicate to repair the house of Jehovah" (I Chr. 26:27).

Solomon, the "man of peace," gathers great numbers of horses and chariots (II Chr. 1:14; 9:25), conquers Hamath-Zobah (II Chr. 8:3), and makes of the children of Israel, not bondservants like the remnant of the Canaanites, but "men of war, and chief of his captains, and rulers of his chariots and of his horsemen" (II Chr. 8:9). The sojourners are numbered and forced to "bear burdens," and to be "hewers in the mountains" for the building of the Temple (II Chr. 2:17-18; 8:7). Tribute is brought to Solomon from "all the kings of the earth" (II Chr. 9:13-14, 23-24), and his dominion "over all the kings from the River even unto the land of the Philistines, and to the border of Egypt" (II Chr. 9:26) is the one sure basis of the much-vaunted peace.

The Chronicler retains from I Samuel the story of David's unfortunate attempt to "show kindness unto Hanum," king of the Ammonites, upon the death of his father—with Hanum's insulting treatment of the messengers, and the resultant brutal war (I Chr. 19:1 to 20:3).

To offset this, we have the friendly relations of David and of Solomon with Huram of Tyre (I Chr. 14:1-2; II Chr. 2:1-16), and of Solomon with the Queen of Sheba (II Chr. 9:1-12). It is noteworthy, too, that in one instance Yahweh speaks to a king of Judah through the Pharaoh of Egypt; Josiah is guilty of sin and is slain in battle for not heeding "the words of Neco from the mouth of God" (II Chr. 35:20-24).

Since everything that happens is considered the result of divine purpose, whoever dies must have been slain by Yahweh, particularly if the death is sudden or spectacular. The Chronicler is more careful than any of his predecessors, however, to justify every divine act of punishment or reward by showing what conduct had merited this treatment. Cultic sins naturally loom large among those requiring drastic punishment.

In spite of its supreme interest in the Temple and all connected with it, we have found in this writing much stress on such points as preparedness for war, Yahweh's help in battle, His use of war as a means of national punishment or discipline, and the conquest of neighboring nations as the way to attain the divine gift of peace. The one suggestion of religious disparagement of bloodshed in war is offset by numerous examples of Yahweh's instigating war and participating in it. In this late document, we find the God of heaven and earth just as exclusively interested in one chosen nation as in writings from an early period of Hebrew history.

JONAH

The story of Jonah was probably written during the early Greek period, three or four centuries after Nineveh had ceased to be a formidable foe of the Hebrew people. Since keen hatred of Nineveh, such as is voiced by Nahum, was thus long past by the time of this writing, its readers could enter without too much feeling into the situation proposed in the story, and instead of being repelled at once, they might read on till they caught the writer's whole meaning. On the other hand, Nineveh would always represent to the Jewish mind, in a rather typical and symbolical way, an enemy and oppressor, and the attitudes valid toward Nineveh would be those suitable toward foes. When the author of this tale caricatured the attitude of Jonah or the Jews in contrast with the attitude of Yahweh, he was striking at conditions in his own day, and seeking to influence a people who were on the whole nationally intolerant and exclusive, convinced not only of the superiority of their race and religion, but also of their special right to Yahweh's care and mercy, with no moral compulsion whatever to share with outsiders the religious heritage produced for them through the spiritual travail of prophets, priests, and sages.

The Yahweh of the author of Jonah is in touch with all nations. He is as conscious of wickedness as is the Yahweh of the prophets of doom, and is under as urgent necessity of vindicating His ethical standards by punishing evil wherever He finds it in the world.[7] His commission to Jonah is: "Arise, go to Nineveh,

[7] Apparently Yahweh's requirements are solely ethical, since it is assumed that the repentant Ninevites are capable of satisfying them without any special instruction.

that great city, and cry against it; for their wickedness is come up before me" (1:2; cf. 3:2, 4).

There is, however, no stress upon the wrath of Yahweh,[8] and the probability lies open, in view of the concluding revelation of Yahweh's attitude, that the necessity of punishing is a grief to Him, that the repeated expression "that great city" carries a note of pathos in its suggestion of the great number of persons who must suffer this punishment, and that Yahweh's hope all the time has been that conversion rather than doom would follow upon the prophet's proclamation.

Twice Yahweh asks Jonah: "Doest thou well to be angry?" (4:4, 9a) Apparently it is not a state of mind that meets with divine approbation.

Jonah's characterization of Yahweh is all the more impressive because of the disgust with which he speaks. "For I knew that thou art a gracious God, and merciful, slow to anger, and abundant in lovingkindness, and repentest thee of the evil" (4:2b). One recalls former descriptions of Yahweh, beginning like this, but ending how differently—"and that will by no means clear the guilty"! (Ex. 34:6-7; Nahum 1:3) The Yahweh of Jonah has become a consistently merciful God, rather than one "forgiving iniquity and transgression and sin" and then in the same breath "visiting the iniquity of the fathers upon the children, and upon the children's children, upon the third and upon the fourth generation" (Ex. 34:7).

This deepened and more consistent mercifulness of Yahweh rests apparently upon a compassionate regard for the worth of the life of every human being. He knows just how many babies there are in the great city of Nineveh, and He cares even for the "much cattle" that would have suffered in the destruction of the city. What is a gourd, or a prophet's reputation for infallibility, or any other consideration of the comfort or prestige of Jonah the Jew, compared with the supreme value of these lives, which, it would seem, Yahweh has "labored for" and "made grow"? (4:10-11)

All the phenomena of nature are evidently under the absolute control of this "God of heaven, who hath made the sea and

[8] The only mention of God's anger is in the proclamation of mourning and moral reform made by the King of Nineveh, and even there it is combined with the hope that God will show mercy (3:9).

the dry land" (1:9), and He continually manipulates them to further His purposes (1:4, 17; 2:10; 4:6-8). But the character of these purposes we have already seen to be in striking contrast to those for which the God of Israel was once thought to use His power over nature, and it is worth noting that at no point in the perilous adventures of Jonah and the mariners does Yahweh allow a life to be lost or even injured.

The major point, Yahweh's attitude toward foreigners, is emphasized by this writer's generously favorable portrayal of the non-Jewish characters throughout the tale. The heathen mariners appear more sensitive than Jonah to Yahweh's dealings (1:5, 13-16), whereas the king and people of Nineveh repent with a unanimity and thoroughness such as was certainly never found among the Hebrews in response to a prophet's message (3:5-8).

The poetic prayer of Jonah from within the fish is clearly not a part of the original story.[9] Its dominant idea, Yahweh's answer to the appeal of one in deep affliction, is in harmony with the character of the Yahweh of the story, but since this is the song of a Jew, who would naturally expect to be answered, it has no special significance.

The author of the story of Jonah has presented with humor and artistic skill a conception of Yahweh which retains the ideas of the God of nature and the God of righteousness, but reinterprets the quality of Yahweh's attitude toward men, and the range of His care. At last Yahweh's loving concern for men reaches all those over whom He exercises dominion. He responds to repentance with compassionate eagerness, for every life is precious to Him. His regard has no national limits; people looked upon as enemies of the Jews are the objects of His solicitude and lovingkindness.

[9] Cf. Bewer, *International Critical Commentary* on *Jonah*, pp. 22 f., 42.

CHAPTER VIII

WISDOM LITERATURE AND POETIC ANTHOLOGIES

1. Job, Proverbs, Ecclesiastes, Song of Songs—2. Psalms—3. Appendix to Discussion of Psalms

THE WISDOM LITERATURE AND THE SONG OF SONGS

If we date Proverbs partly during the Persian and partly during the Greek period,[1] Job about 400 B.C.,[2] and Ecclesiastes about 200 B.C.,[3] the lack of Jewish national independence or of any hope of regaining it may be a large factor in the development of the "wisdom" type of literature, with its almost complete absence of national consciousness, and its concentration on some of the most common problems of thought and conduct of individual human beings.

The Song of Songs shares this characteristic of the wisdom literature, and was probably compiled in this same general period, perhaps in the third century B.C.[4]

JOB

It is significant that the hero of the book of Job is not a Jew, but "a man in the land of Uz, . . . the greatest of all the children of the east." Job's friends, likewise, are non-Jewish. The book, then, is to deal with a broadly human problem, rather than with a problem of the Jews as such.

This universalistic outlook, as we have just indicated, goes hand in hand with the focusing of interest upon the individual, rather than upon the nation as a unit. Hence, in the book of Job we shall have no occasion to find indications of God's partiality for one nation over against another. The nature of its problem and the nationality of its characters carry the assumption of divine impartiality.

[1] Cf. Bewer, *The Literature of the Old Testament*, p. 309.
[2] *Ibid.*, p. 317.
[3] *Ibid.*, p. 330.
[4] *Ibid.*, p. 393.

Wisdom Literature and Poetic Anthologies 137

It is occasionally suggested in the book that God's dealings with different nations are of the same tenor as His dealings with individuals. Job asserts that just as God's wisdom and might enable Him utterly to confound all sorts of individual men, so also

> He increaseth the nations, and he destroyeth them:
> He enlargeth the nations, and he leadeth them captive.
> He taketh away understanding from the chiefs of the people of the earth,
> And causeth them to wander in a wilderness where there is no way. (12: 23-24; cf. 34: 29)

The phase of our investigation, then, which this book touches most is the question as to God's attitude toward men in general. On this we have in the main two conflicting views—that of Job, in his desperation, and that of his friends, in their smug orthodoxy.

Only a few typical quotations are needed to make clear the orthodox view of Job's friends. The righteous are showered with blessings and protected from the wicked.

> But he saveth from the sword of their mouth,
> Even the needy from the hand of the mighty. (5: 15)

A man may, however, need disciplinary punishment, in which case God chastises and then blesses.

> For he maketh sore, and bindeth up;
> He woundeth, and his hands make whole. (5: 18)

The individual thus reinstated in God's favor is the object of His unlimited protective power.

> He will deliver thee in six troubles;
> Yea, in seven there shall no evil touch thee.
> In famine he will redeem thee from death;
> And in war from the power of the sword. (5: 19-20)

Though the disciplinary conception is thus introduced in the first speech of Eliphaz, and is touched elsewhere, particularly in the Elihu interpolation [5] (e.g., 33: 15-28), on the whole this

[5] The Elihu speeches, chs. 32-37, are not generally considered a part of the original poem.

idea is much less prominent than the idea of destructive punishment. The thoroughly wicked are uprooted, are consumed, they perish forever.

> According as I have seen, they that plow iniquity,
> And sow trouble, reap the same.
> By the breath of God they perish,
> And by the blast of his anger are they consumed. (4:8-9)

(Cf. 5:3-5; 8:13-22; 15:20-35; 18:5-21; 20:4-29; 34:21-28; 36:6, 12.)

Job, on the other hand, in the agony of his suffering, sees in God the relentless and unaccountable tormentor of the righteous, or the comparatively righteous.

> For the arrows of the Almighty are within me,
> The poison whereof my spirit drinketh up:
> The terrors of God do set themselves in array against me. (6:4)

> If I have sinned, what do I unto thee, O thou watcher of men?
> Why hast thou set me as a mark for thee,
> So that I am a burden to myself?
> And why dost thou not pardon my transgression, and take away mine iniquity? (7:20-21a)

> Behold, he seizeth the prey, who can hinder him?
> Who will say unto him, What doest thou? (9:12)

> It is all one; therefore I say,
> He destroyeth the perfect and the wicked. (9:22)

(Cf. 9:17-19, 30-35; 10:2-3, 14-17, 20; 13:15, 21; 14:13; 16:11-14; 19:6-22; 30:20-23.)

This is the idea most common in Job's complaints, though at times he seems to fall back on the righteous God of his past thought and experience as a sort of court of appeal from the divine torturer of his present experience.

The God of the speeches by Yahweh (chs. 38-41) is incomprehensible, all-wise, and all-powerful. Man should regard Him with humility and awe.

Or hast thou an arm like God?
And canst thou thunder with a voice like him? (40:9)

The Yahweh of the prose prologue and epilogue is quite an anthropomorphic Being, willing to permit a paragon of righteousness to be subjected to excruciating torture in order to vindicate His boast to Satan—and then, once Job has passed the test for disinterested goodness, piling blessings upon him.

Varied as are the conceptions of God presented in the book, they have in common the idea that God's power is absolute, and that He may use it to destructive ends, whether only against the wicked or with irresponsible enmity against any whom He may choose to harass.[6]

PROVERBS

The book of Proverbs comprises a number of smaller collections, which when assembled make a rather heterogeneous array. Since the ideas that here concern us appear, however, fairly consistently, we may deal with the book as a whole.

Though the sages use in Proverbs the proper name "Yahweh," they are not presenting nationalistic aspects of His attitude. The thought of this book, like that of the other wisdom literature, is focused upon universal problems of human life, arising out of the relations of any individual with his fellows and with a higher Power.

All nations seem to be regarded on the same plane in the observation:

Righeousness exalteth a nation;
But sin is a reproach to any people. (14:34)

Yet there are frequent indications that the writers of Proverbs are thinking of individuals' relations just to their neighbors within the community, and are not including in their view possible neighborly relations with other peoples.

[6] Though God thus shows no leniency toward those whom He seems to account His enemies, we should note one striking factor in Job's description of his own righteous conduct, supposedly approved by God:
  If I have rejoiced at the destruction of him that hated me,
  Or lifted up myself when evil found him
  (Yea, I have not suffered my mouth to sin
  By asking his life with a curse). (31:29-30)

War is assumed:

Every purpose is established by counsel;
And by wise guidance make thou war. (20:18; cf. 24:6)

The horse is prepared against the day of battle;
But victory is of Jehovah. (21:31)

Foreigners seem to be regarded with suspicion:

Take his garment that is surety for a stranger;
And hold him in pledge that is surety for foreigners. (20:16
cf. 27:13)

The expressions "the strange woman," "the foreigner," or "the foreign woman," usually are synonyms for a harlot. (Cf. 2:16; 5:3, 20; 7:5; 22:14; 23:27.)

Yahweh's attitude toward other peoples is not given explicitly. Of course, "the foreigner" in the sense given above would incur the punishment which He metes out to the wicked.

The dire fate of the wicked sometimes appears like just an inevitable natural result of wrongdoing, but elsewhere it is made clear that Yahweh is the immediate cause of their calamity.

For the backsliding of the simple shall slay them,
And the careless ease of fools shall destroy them. (1:32)

But the wicked shall be cut off from the land,
And the treacherous shall be rooted out of it. (3:22)

Jehovah hath made everything for its own end;
Yea, even the wicked for the day of evil. (16:4)

The curse of Jehovah is in the house of the wicked;
 *   *   *   *   *   *
Surely he scoffeth at the scoffers. (3:33a, 34a)

(Cf. 4:19; 6:15; 10:25, 27-32; 11:18-21, 23; 12:2-3; 14:11-12; etc.) Yahweh's scoffing at the wicked when they are undone reminds one of Wisdom's mocking laughter when anguish overtakes those who have refused to regard her (1:26-29).

Far different from the lot of the wicked is the reward of the righteous.

He layeth up sound wisdom for the upright;
He is a shield to them that walk in integrity;
That he may guard the paths of justice,
And preserve the way of his saints. (2:7-8)

The path of the righteous is as the dawning light,
That shineth more and more unto the perfect day. (4:18)

The name of Jehovah is a strong tower;
The righteous runneth into it, and is safe. (18:10)

(Cf. 3:32-34; 10:2-3, 6-9, 25, 27-32; 11:18-21, 23, 31; 13:21; etc.)

On the whole, the righteous and the wicked, or the wise and the foolish, are treated in Proverbs like two different species. There seems little chance for the wicked to become righteous.

He that correcteth a scoffer getteth to himself reviling;
And he that reproveth a wicked man getteth himself a blot.
Reprove not a scoffer, lest he hate thee:
Reprove a wise man, and he will love thee. (9:7-8)

Speak not in the hearing of a fool;
For he will despise the wisdom of thy words. (23:9)

Yet there seems to be a stage before the individual is irrevocably consigned to either of these classes, or a time when the potentially wise are in danger of acting foolishly. The chief object of the maxims must be to prevent one who has the power of choice from becoming wicked. For those, moreover, who have not committed themselves too far to evil and folly, some of the sages believe in the efficacy of punishment for reclamation. When He chastises such, Yahweh has a loving rather than a destructive purpose.

My son, despise not the chastening of Jehovah;
Neither be weary of his reproof:
For whom Jehovah loveth he reproveth,
Even as a father the son in whom he delighteth. (3:11-12)

Stripes that wound cleanse away evil;
And strokes reach the innermost parts. (20:30)

By mercy and truth iniquity is atoned for;
And by the fear of Jehovah men depart from evil. (16:6)

Within the community, strife is to be avoided, and the attitudes which would engender strife are continually inveighed against.

> Hatred stirreth up strifes,
> But love covereth all transgressions. (10:12; cf. 10:18; 15:17; 26:24-26)

Vexation should be concealed. (12:16; 15:1; 17:9, 14, 19; 18:19)

> The discretion of a man maketh him slow to anger;
> And it is his glory to pass over a transgression. (19:11)

Anger is the source of a vast amount of evil.

> He that is slow to anger is better than the mighty;
> And he that ruleth his spirit, than he that taketh a city. (16:32)
>
> An angry man stirreth up strife,
> And a wrathful man aboundeth in transgression. (29:22)

(Cf. 14:17a, 29; 15:18; 19:19a; 20:3; 22:24; 27:4; 29:11; 30:33.) Yahweh hates "him that soweth discord among brethren" (6:19b), but "to the counsellors of peace is joy" (12:20).

Kindness is one's duty to one's fellows, but only a qualified kindness. One who obviously deserves it should be treated kindly (3:27, 30). But what of one's dealings with his enemies in the community? To them, too, kindness should often be shown—but for a purely prudential motive, for the sake of its effect on Yahweh, in keeping Him favorable to the one who acts kindly, and hostile to his enemies.

> Rejoice not when thine enemy falleth,
> And let not thy heart be glad when he is overthrown;
> Lest Jehovah see it, and it displease him,
> And he turn away his wrath from him. (24:17-18)
>
> If thine enemy be hungry, give him bread to eat;
> And if he be thirsty, give him water to drink:
> For thou wilt heap coals of fire upon his head,
> And Jehovah will reward thee. (25:21-22)

After all, the best means of pacifying enemies, as of worsting them, is Yahweh's favor.

When a man's ways please Jehovah,
He maketh even his enemies to be at peace with him. (16:7)

The Yahweh of Proverbs, we have seen, influences human life mainly through His function of rewarding the righteous and overwhelming the wicked. To be "righteous" in His eyes requires certain conduct and attitudes toward one's neighbors which, if extended to all men everywhere, might go far to do away with all strife, but the book of Proverbs neither frees such conduct of its prudential motive for the individual, nor suggests its applicability within a wider sphere than the community or the nation.

ECCLESIASTES

The book of Koheleth, or Ecclesiastes, is not in detail relevant to our investigation, but its general viewpoint should be noted.

Like the other wisdom literature, this book is dealing with human life per se, with no particularistic bias. Even the sage's assumption of the rôle of King Solomon introduces no nationalistic touch, since the character is significant here only as the embodiment of unexampled wisdom and unlimited opportunity for life's supposedly richest experiences.

The God of the "gentle cynic" is far off somewhere, incomprehensible, responsible for the world order but failing to give any indication of purposeful direction of it. Human life, therefore, is a meaningless round. "All is vanity and a striving after wind." Regardless of what men do, "time and chance happeneth to them all" (9:11b). Human effort cannot gain significance by being linked to great divine purposes, for the God of Koheleth is not in earnest.

Against the background of this dominant idea, it is easy to detect the interpolations which present the orthodox conception of a God who rewards the good and punishes the wicked (cf. 2:26; 3:17; 8:12-13; 12:13-14).[7]

[7] Since apothegms from this book have frequently appealed to religious educators as useful for memory verses, it may be pertinent to note a few which seem to bear directly or indirectly on the question of attitudes toward war.
The list of illustrations of "a time for every purpose" ends: "a time for war, and a time for peace" (3:8 b). War is assumed as a part of life in the illustration of another point (8:8 c).

144 *The God of the Old Testament in Relation to War*

SONG OF SONGS

This anthology of love and marriage songs has deep human significance and a broad human appeal. The nature of its subject relieves it of any nationalistic coloring.

The poems do not deal with the nature or character of the deity, except when misinterpreted as allegorical, and there is no occasion for the expression of attitudes toward war.[8]

PSALMS

The Psalter is an anthology of religious poetry covering a period of nearly a thousand years, and hence reflecting a wide range of historical situations out of which the kingdom of Israel or the later Jewish community calls upon its God. A great number of individuals, moreover, with different types of experience and tendencies of thought, here voice their personal reactions to these varying conditions, with the freedom of self-revelation afforded by prayer.

The original poems, even if chronologically arranged, would offer a bewildering variety of conceptions of Yahweh, but when we add to these considerations the fact that the date of most of the psalms is uncertain, that they have neither chronological nor topical arrangement, and that almost all of them have been worked over by one or more editors, whose views often disagree with those of the first writers, the problem of discussing the conception of God in the Psalter is seen to be still more difficult.

Obviously, we cannot expect to find wholly consistent ideas. In this study, we shall merely attempt to discover what different conceptions, relevant to our problem, are present in the Psalter, and which of these are particularly frequent.

The Yahweh of the psalmists is a God capable of working His will completely.

The story of the poor wise man who delivered a besieged city is followed by the maxim: "Wisdom is better than weapons of war" (9:18 a).

Another set of maxims (7:8 b-9) exalts patience and the restraint of anger, but doubtless, like Proverbs, has in view only the relations between individuals in the community.

[8] War is, of course, a part of the writers' experience of life, and so may be drawn upon for illustrative imagery (3:7-8; 4:4; 6:4, 10).

All nature is in awe of Him and under His dominion (29; 68:7-9; 114; et al.). Some of the most beautiful of the psalms are devoted to an expression of reverent admiration for the Creator's revelation of Himself in nature (19:1-6; 65:9-13; 104; 147, *passim*). Psalm 8 (except vs. 2) combines this thought with grateful wonder at the place of dignity assigned to mankind in creation. To Yahweh belong heaven and earth (89:11-12; 24:1) and He is inescapably present in every part of the universe (139:7-12).

Yahweh not only controls physical nature, but He reigns over all nations, according to many of the psalms (22:28; 46:10; 47:2, 7-9; 93; 97; 99; 103:19; 113:4). Frequently He appears as the righteous judge of the nations (7:8a; 9:5, 7-8, 15-20; 82:8; 96; 98).

A step beyond this conception of Yahweh's universal dominion is reached in those passages which conceive of Yahweh as worshipped and praised by all nations.

All the ends of the earth shall remember and turn unto Jehovah;
And all the kindreds of the nations shall worship before thee. (22:27)

O thou that hearest prayer,
Unto thee shall all flesh come. (65:2)

(Cf. 66:4; 67; 86:9; 96; 98; 100; 102:22; 117.) The whole creation is summoned to praise Yahweh in Psalm 148, and the Psalter closes with a praise symphony from which no living being is excluded:

Let everything that hath breath praise Jehovah.
Praise ye Jehovah. (150:6)

In most cases, this worship and praise from all men seems to be a voluntary response to Yahweh for beneficent acts toward them, but sometimes it is, rather, homage arising from awe at manifestations of His great power (e.g., 66:1-4). Occasionally, we find the definite assertion that His care or lovingkindness extends to all men (33:5; 36:7; 145:8-18, 21).

146 *The God of the Old Testament in Relation to War*

This universalistic spirit, though so often found either in the original psalms or in glosses, is, however, not characteristic of the book of Psalms as a whole. We have here, as a rule, the hymns of a people addressed to the God who belongs peculiarly to them; they are concerned with His relation to them and to their enemies, or else they are prayers of individuals in danger or distress who seek divine help and protection for themselves.

Yahweh's "lovingkindness" is repeatedly demonstrated to individuals or to the nation by the destruction of adversaries.

> My God with his lovingkindness will meet me:
> God will let me see my desire upon mine enemies. (59:10)

(Cf. 17:7; 31:15-17; 40; 54:7; 57:3; 59:10, 13; 69:16-18; 89:23-24; 92; 107:1-3; 118; 136; 138:7-8; 143:12.) The fighting saints of Psalm 149:5-9 are worth noting in this connection.

> Let the saints exult in glory:
> Let them sing for joy upon their beds.
> Let the high praises of God be in their mouth,
> And a two-edged sword in their hand;
> To execute vengeance upon the nations,
> And punishments upon the peoples;
> To bind their kings with chains,
> And their nobles with fetters of iron;
> To execute upon them the judgment written:
> This honor have all his saints.

Of all the themes in the Psalter, the most common is Yahweh's overthrow of the enemies of the psalmist, who often, perhaps usually, is speaking on behalf of the nation or the restored Jewish community. Sometimes Yahweh's destruction of the speaker's foes has already been accomplished (3; 9:3-6; 18:1-3, 13-19, 46-48; 27:1-3, 6; 92:11), but much more frequently the assurance of Yahweh's partisanship is felt to justify vigorous imprecation against present enemies or an assertion of Yahweh's certain vengeance upon them.

> Arise, O Jehovah, in thine anger;
> Lift up thyself against the rage of mine adversaries,
> And awake for me; thou hast commanded judgment. (7:6)

Strive thou, O Jehovah, with them that strive with me:
Fight thou against them that fight against me.
Take hold of shield and buckler,
And stand up for my help.
Draw out also the spear, and stop the way against them that pursue me:
Say unto my soul, I am thy salvation.
Let them be put to shame and brought to dishonor that seek after my soul:
Let them be turned back and confounded that devise my hurt.
Let them be as chaff before the wind,
And the angel of Jehovah driving them on.
Let their way be dark and slippery,
And the angel of Jehovah pursuing them.
For without cause have they hid for me their net in a pit;
Without cause have they digged a pit for my soul.
Let destruction come upon him unawares;
And let his net that he hath hid catch himself:
With destruction let him fall therein.
And my soul shall be joyful in Jehovah:
It shall rejoice in his salvation. (35:1-9)

Let the wicked fall into their own nets,
Whilst that I withal escape. (141:10)

Through God we shall do valiantly,
For he it is that will tread down our adversaries. (60:12 or 108:13)

(Cf. 5:10; 6:8-10; 17:7-9, 13; 25:2, 19-20; 28:4-5; 31:15-18; 35:17, 22-23, 26; 38:15, 19-22; 40:14-17; 41:10-11; 54:5; 55:9, 15, 23; 56:1-2, 7, 9; 58:6-9; 59; 63:9-11; 64:7-8; 69:22-28; 70; 71:12-13; 109:6-15; 120; 129:4-7; 137:7-9; 138:7; 140; 142:6; 143:9; 144:5-7.)

In numerous instances, Yahweh is portrayed as fighting, or about to fight, against His own enemies.

Thy hand will find out all thine enemies;
Thy right hand will find out those that hate thee.
Thou wilt make them as a fiery furnace in the time of thine anger:
Jehovah will swallow them up in his wrath,
And the fire shall devour them.

148 The God of the Old Testament in Relation to War

Their fruit wilt thou destroy from the earth,
And their seed from among the children of men.
For they intended evil against thee;
They conceived a device which they are not able to perform.
For thou wilt make ready with thy bowstrings against their face.
Be thou exalted, O Jehovah, in thy strength:
So will we sing and praise thy power. (21: 8-13)

Let God arise, let his enemies be scattered;
Let them also that hate him flee before him.
As smoke is driven away, so drive them away:
As wax melteth before the fire,
So let the wicked perish at the presence of God. (68: 1-2)

(Cf. 8:2; 10:16; 14:4-5; 53:4-5; 66:3; 68:21-23; 74:4, 10-11, 18, 22-23; 79:12-13; 83; 89:8, 10, 13; 92:9; 94:1-3; 97:3.) It would be difficult to find a more caustic expression of a god's contempt for other peoples than the one in Psalm 60: 7-8 (or 108: 8-9):

Gilead is mine, and Manasseh is mine;
Ephraim also is the defence of my head;
Judah is my sceptre.
Moab is my washpot;
Upon Edom will I cast my shoe:
Philistia, shout thou because of me.

Sometimes the ones whom Yahweh will destroy are the enemies of His anointed king.

Jehovah said unto my Lord, Sit thou at my right hand,
Until I make thine enemies thy footstool.
Jehovah will send forth the rod of thy strength out of Zion:
Rule thou in the midst of thine enemies. (110: 1-2)

(Cf. 2; 110: 5-6; 132: 18.) The ideal king in Psalm 72 will be utterly gracious and just toward his own people, but the other nations will grovel before him (72: 8-11).[9]

The conception of Yahweh's fighting leads now and then to vivid descriptions of the mighty warrior-god.

---

[9] Dominion over others is thought of in other passages, also, as one of the blessings bestowed by Yahweh upon His favored ones (18: 43-45, 47; 47: 3-4).

Wisdom Literature and Poetic Anthologies

If a man turn not, he will whet his sword;
He hath bent his bow, and made it ready;
He hath also prepared for him the instruments of death;
He maketh his arrows fiery shafts. (7:12-13)

Who is the King of glory?
Jehovah strong and mighty,
Jehovah mighty in battle. (24:8)

(Cf. 17:13; 18:6-14; 35:1-3; 47:5; 78:65-66.)

As a means of assuring themselves that Yahweh will subdue their present enemies, the psalmists like to recall His destruction of Israel's adversaries in the past. (Cf. 22:4-5; 44:2-3; 48:4-8; 78:49-55; 80:8; 83:9-12; 105:24-38, 44; 106:10-11; 124:2-3, 6; 135:8-12.)

Yahweh is the source of the personal prowess of a victorious warrior (18:34-39; 144:1-2), and the one who always determines which side shall conquer in battle (18:40-42). Chariots and horses and armaments are needless with Him (20:5-9; 33:16-17, 20; 44:5-7; 147:10), and they are impotent against Him (20:7; 46:9; 76:3, 5-7).

With such a conception of Yahweh's power, any calamity, either personal or national, must be the result of Yahweh's anger or neglect.

O God, thou hast cast us off, thou hast broken us down;
Thou hast been angry; oh restore us again.

* * * * * *

Hast thou not, O God, cast us off?
And thou goest not forth, O God, with our hosts. (60:1, 10)

(Cf. 6; 13:1-2; 22:1-2; 27:9; 38:1, 3; 39:10; 44:9-10; 74:1; 77:9; 78:21-22, 30-31, 58-64; 79:5-7; 80:4-7; 85:5; 88:7, 16; 89:38-46; 90:7, 9, 11; 95:8-11; 102:1-11; 106:17-18, 23, 26-41.)

In most of the psalms that express fear or hostility, the enemies of the psalmist or of the praying community are explicitly identified with "the wicked" (e.g., 3:7*bc*; 5:8-10; 6:7-8; 9:3-5; 17:9; 28:3-4; 31:15, 17; 36:11-12; 56:7-9; 71:4; 94).

Certain psalms which suggest that enemies are in the background are capable of being adapted to other situations because the dominant note is the psalmist's peace and trust in Yahweh's care or protection, rather than active animosity. Such are Psalms 4 (see vss. 2, 4), 16 (see vs. 1), 23 (vs. 5a), 61 (vs. 3), 62 (vss. 3-4), and 86 (vss. 14, 17). Psalms 42-43 mainly express deep longing for the realization of God that comes in the Temple worship, and assurance that the hope of help from Yahweh will eventually be fulfilled; oppressing enemies are mentioned without imprecation in 42: 9-10 and 43: 1-2.

Enemies have dropped out of view still more in Psalm 84, where the conventional epithets "Jehovah of hosts" and "God our shield" are the only reminders, and in Psalm 91, where we have, however, a divine "refuge" and "fortress," "shield and buckler," reference to "the terror by night" and "the arrow that flieth by day," and a deepening of the writer's sense of security by contrast with the destruction of those who are without his refuge (vss. 7-8). In Psalm 121 Yahweh will "keep" Israel, and in Psalm 125 His protective presence is round about His people, but there is no reference to any particular danger threatening them. Psalm 131 gives humble, childlike trust with no suggestion of enemies.

Some fairly long passages seem originally to have celebrated Yahweh's lovingkindness without association with the idea of the destruction of enemies, but it is noteworthy that now this thought is usually found with them. Examples would be 36: 5-10, to which vss. 11-12 may have been added later; and 63: 1-8, with vss. 9-11 added. Psalm 107 suggests adversaries only in vss. 2-3, and Psalm 111, in vs. 6. Psalm 116 seems entirely free from the idea.

Yahweh is frequently represented as a God ready to pardon Israel or the individual psalmist. In the past, He has shown His people mercy and forgiveness (78: 38; 85: 1-3). Confessions of sin or pleas for pardon indicate the conception of a forgiving God (25: 7, 11, 18; 40: 12; 51: 1-12). Joy and gratitude for the present forgiveness of sin are sometimes expressed (32: 1, 5; 103: 8-13), or sure conviction that Yahweh will forgive (65: 3; 130: 3-4, 7-8).

The idea of Yahweh's forgiveness of any but the speakers is, however, almost impossible to find. The conception in 51:13 seems to be unique:

> Then will I teach transgressors thy ways;
> And sinners shall be converted unto thee.

The more usual thought is that contempt or hatred toward the wicked is pleasing to Yahweh.

> Do not I hate them, O Jehovah, that hate thee?
> And am not I grieved with those that rise up against thee?
> I hate them with perfect hatred:
> They are become mine enemies. (139:21-22)

(Cf. 15:4a; 26:5; 31:6; 101:5, 8; 119:113.)

Yahweh Himself apparently hates the wicked, in most of the psalms, and does not contemplate their conversion. The contrast between Yahweh's blessing for the righteous and destruction for the wicked is a favorite theme, the treatment of the wicked culminating in punishment rather than redemption.

> Jehovah trieth the righteous;
> But the wicked and him that loveth violence his soul hateth.
> Upon the wicked he will rain snares;
> Fire and brimstone and burning wind shall be the portion of
>   their cup.
> For Jehovah is righteous; he loveth righteousness:
> The upright shall behold his face. (11:5-7)

(Cf. 1; 5:5-6, 10-12; 7; 12; 34; 37 (especially vss. 10-11, 13, 15, 17, 20, 28, 34); 49; 50; 52; 73:18-20, 27; 75:8, 10; 92:7-15; 112; 119; 145:20; 146; 147:6.)

Occasionally we catch a glimpse of the derisive joy of the righteous at the destruction of the wicked:

> The righteous shall rejoice when he seeth the vengeance:
> He shall wash his feet in the blood of the wicked;
> So that men shall say, Verily, there is a reward for the
>   righteous:
> Verily there is a God that judgeth the earth. (58:10-11; cf.
>   52:6-7)

In Psalm 73:23-26, fellowship with God is adequate consolation for the innocent sufferer, but it is exceptional to find satisfaction without the orthodox assurance of direct divine reward and retribution, and even this passage is now enclosed in others that forcefully state the idea that Yahweh eventually casts the wicked down to destruction (73:17-20, 27).

From this survey it appears that, although universalistic ideas are present in a considerable number of instances, the God portrayed in the Psalms is usually either the militant henotheistic deity of the Hebrew people or that more powerful but equally partisan God who controls both nature and all history in the interests of one nation. He fights and destroys His own enemies, either hostile nations or the wicked within Israel, and, except when He is temporarily angry, His might is at the service of His favored ones against their enemies.

APPENDIX TO DISCUSSION OF PSALMS

Although the psalms are rarely made the central teaching material for the lesson period, their use as auxiliary material, either in teaching or in worship, is so extensive as to give them vital importance in such an investigation as this. As used in religious education for reading or study or memorization, the psalms are selected individually, and the educator's interest thus centers in the value of specific psalms, rather than of the collection as a whole. It has therefore seemed desirable to add here some comments on the ideas found in certain of the psalms most used now and a few others suitable for use by those who desire to promote peace-making attitudes.

Psalm 1

In the introductory psalm, dating from the Greek period, the two contrasted groups are the ''righteous'' and the ''wicked'' within Israel. Yahweh's treatment of the wicked culminates in punishment rather than redemption. Their company is to be shunned by the righteous; they will be blown away like chaff, and will have no part in the resurrection at the judgment day.

Psalm 2

This Messianic psalm, or ''victorious ode,'' of uncertain date, presents the relation of Yahweh to His enemies, the nations that seek to break away from His domination. Secure in His power, He will greet their efforts with derisive laughter, and give abundant evidence of His wrath. All the nations will be handed over

Wisdom Literature and Poetic Anthologies 153

to His son, the anointed, to be broken "with a rod of iron" and dashed in pieces. Rebellion is useless. The part of wisdom is to follow the dictates of fear and keep in His favor, to avoid His relentless anger.

Psalm 8

The mood of this psalm is one of reverent admiration for the Creator's glory, and for the place given to man in the universe— to mankind as such, not specifically to any one people.
Only in verse 2 occurs an oddly discordant note:

> Out of the mouths of babes and sucklings hast thou established strength,
> Because of thine adversaries,
> That thou mightest still the enemy and the avenger.

Psalm 19

We have here the response to God's revelation of His glory in the heavens, succeeded by a deep and inclusive realization of Yahweh's revelation of Himself in His law, culminating in the writer's sense of liability to sin, and desire to be kept free from it—a psalm that offers a respite from the moods of self-righteousness and animosity so commonly found.

Might the "law of Yahweh" become as precious to other peoples as to Israel? Would Yahweh be to them, also, a "rock" and a "redeemer"? The psalmist does not tell us; doubtless such questions were not within the range of his thought—but we may rejoice that his words do not explicitly preclude the possibility.

Psalm 23

In this, perhaps the best loved of all the psalms, we find a quiet mood of trust and gratitude. The God of this psalmist shows toward him only tender care, "goodness and lovingkindness." As for Yahweh's attitude toward the speaker's enemies, we have just one hint—"Thou preparest a table before me in the presence of mine enemies" (vs. 5a). The complete picture of the divine care for one individual or group seemed to need that!

Psalm 24

Though "the world, and they that dwell therein" belong to Yahweh, probably only Israelites would be expected to fulfil the requirements given for standing in His holy place. This is made more explicit by rendering vs. 6b with Briggs, "Those who seek His face are Jacob."

The first half of the psalm, vss. 1-6, building as it does upon the ethical ideas of the prophets, is much later than the second half, which is plausibly considered to come from the time of David, when the ark was brought into Jerusalem. We are surely in the presence of such a warlike God as was known to David's time:

> Jehovah strong and mighty,
> Jehovah mighty in battle. (vs. 8bc)
> . . .
> Jehovah of hosts,
> He is the King of glory. (vs. 10bc)

Psalms 42-43 (originally one)

Yearning for the realization of God that comes with the Temple worship is the burden of this cry out of exile. Though suffering "the oppression of the enemy" and distressed by their taunts, the writer indulges in no imprecations, but gives only his own struggle against despondency and his assurance that his hope of help from his God will at last be realized.

Psalm 46

The God against whom the nations are helpless (vs. 6), and who is to be recognized as the disposer of all, and exalted throughout the world (vs. 10), is nevertheless still "Jehovah of hosts," "with us," the "God of Jacob," who is the peculiar refuge of His own people.

Of special interest is the assertion in vs. 9a, "He maketh wars to cease unto the end of the earth," but it seems to be because by His might He reduces to futility the nations' implements of war, rather than because He will bring about any condition of international equity and understanding.

Psalm 51

Out of deep humility and contrition comes this cry for divine mercy and forgiveness—this longing for purity of thought and life. To be delivered from "bloodguiltiness" would bring a song of joyous relief.

Not only is the psalm free from any note of hatred toward others; in the one place where sinners other than the writer are mentioned, it is with the thought of converting them, rather than either standing aloof or seeking their punishment.

> Then will I teach transgressors thy ways;
> And sinners shall be converted unto thee. (vs. 13)

Apparently Yahweh wants this, for it is to be done as an evidence of gratitude to Him for His merciful restoration.

Psalm 67

God's blessing upon Israel is for the purpose of making Him known to all nations, who will come to rejoice in His beneficent control. Though this little psalm does not touch upon the nation's mission through suffering, and seems to come from a time of friendliness with other nations, the idea of drawing other peoples to God by their observation of Israel's experience (vss. 1-4) recalls Deutero-Isaiah. "All the ends of the earth shall fear him" (vs. 7b), evidently with joyful reverence, rather than with the terrified submission found in some other psalms.

Wisdom Literature and Poetic Anthologies

Psalm 84

This pilgrim song of deep longing for the Temple worship, and joy in the thought of Yahweh's blessing to those who find Him there, has no trace of militant spirit, though it retains the epithet "Jehovah of hosts" and speaks of Him as a "shield."

Psalm 91

This matchless expression of trust in Yahweh's protection enhances the sense of safety by contrast with the danger of those who are without the divine refuge.

> A thousand shall fall at thy side,
> And ten thousand at thy right hand:
> But it shall not come nigh thee.
> Only with thine eyes shalt thou behold,
> And see the reward of the wicked. (vss. 7-8)

Psalms 96, 98, 100

From the mighty hymn of praise for Yahweh's advent to judge all peoples (Psalms 93 and 96-100), these parts may be selected as most usable. The universal element in Yahweh's relationships is dominant throughout. His lovingkindness and faithfulness to Israel evoke special thanksgiving, but all the earth seems to share the experience of His righteousness and truth and salvation. Not only all mankind, but all physical nature, should participate in the joyous reception of the King.

Psalm 103

Yahweh's attitude toward "them that fear Him" is the sole theme here, so only His mercies and His lovingkindness appear. He is a God who in pity forgives the sin of frail man (vss. 8-13) and who has universal sovereignty (vs. 19).

Psalm 104

This poem celebrates Yahweh's creative power and His wondrous care for all his creatures without a single particularistic or vindictive note, until the discordant gloss in the last verse—

> Let sinners be consumed out of the earth,
> And let the wicked be no more. (35*ab*)

Psalm 116

This psalm contains no mention of enemies or the wicked (except the mild suggestion in vs. 11) or of Yahweh's wrath. Having been preserved from death, through Yahweh's mercy, the writer comes eagerly to offer thanks and pay his vows in the Temple. If the psalm has national significance as well, its freedom from exultation over defeated foes is all the more remarkable.

Psalm 117

This tiny psalm breathes a spirit of generous universalism.

> O praise Jehovah, all ye nations;
> Laud him, all ye peoples.
> For his lovingkindness is great toward us. (vss. 1-2*a*)

If Briggs is right in saying that in vs. 2a "the psalmist combines other nations, whom he addresses, with Israel in personal relation to Yahweh, as the recipients of his kindness and faithfulness,"[10] we reach here one of the highest points in the Psalter.

Psalm 121

This exquisite little hymn of trust does not indicate in any way what Yahweh's "keeping" Israel involves for other nations.

Psalm 122

In this song expressing the pilgrims' happy pride in Jerusalem and prayer for her prosperity, "the peace of Jerusalem" is the greatest good sought. Whether the peace would be shared by others, and how, is not suggested.

Psalm 139

In this psalm, as it now stands, a meditation upon the wonder of Yahweh's inescapable presence and His all-encompassing knowledge of man's nature and purposes is succeeded by a passage in quite different vein, where Yahweh is represented as a slayer of the wicked, to whom hatred of the wicked by His devotee is pleasing (vss. 19, 21-22). It is most revealing to find this avowal of "perfect hatred" followed by a prayer for God to search the heart "and see if there be any wicked way in me."

Psalm 145

The mighty works and gracious providence of Yahweh which call forth praise in this psalm seem free from any nationalistic limitation whatever.

> Jehovah is gracious, and merciful;
> Slow to anger, and of great lovingkindness.
> Jehovah is good to all;
> And his tender mercies are over all his works.
>
> . . .
>
> Thou openest thy hand,
> And satisfiest the desire of every living thing.
>
> . . .
>
> Jehovah is nigh unto all them that call upon him,
> To all that call upon him in truth.   (vss. 8-9, 16, 18)

Yahweh is still, however, a God who destroys the wicked (vs. 20).

Psalm 148

Yahweh's praise is enjoined upon all nature and all mankind, including

> Kings of the earth and all peoples;
> Princes and all judges of the earth.

He is, nevertheless, especially close to one people (vs. 14).

Psalm 150

"Everything that hath breath" is summoned to join the symphony of praise to Yahweh.

[10] Cf. Briggs, *International Critical Commentary* on *Psalms*, Vol. II, p. 402.

CHAPTER IX

PROPHECY FROM THE SECOND CENTURY

1. Daniel—2. Other Prophecies from the Second Century

DANIEL

The profanation of the Temple by order of Antiochus Epiphanes in 168 B.C., and the succeeding persecution of the Jews, ushered in some of the most troublous days that the people of Yahweh had ever known. The victories of Judas Maccabæus and his little band of the faithful brought a gleam of hope, but it seemed almost impossible that they could achieve permanent relief from the oppressions of Syria. Nowhere on the horizon appeared any adequate human aid. Would Yahweh allow his own to be crushed, without intervening on their behalf? A writer convinced of Yahweh's power to save them and His purpose to do so strove to inspire the sufferers with his own assurance, through stories of how Yahweh had most marvelously protected His faithful worshippers in the past, and through visions presaging the imminent downfall of Syria and the rescue of the "saints of the Most High."

In the book of Daniel, Yahweh is in complete control of the fortunes of all nations. "He removeth kings and setteth up kings" (2:21b; cf. 1:2; 2:37-38, 44). The fact, also, that God continually reveals to Daniel what will happen to the nations in the days to come implies His power to direct events to a happy outcome.

It is essential that this control by Yahweh should be universally recognized. He shapes His treatment of men "to the intent that the living may know that the Most High ruleth in the kingdom of men, and giveth it to whomsoever he will" (4:17; cf. 4:25b). As for Nebuchadnezzar, "thy kingdom shall be sure unto thee, after that thou shalt have known that the heavens do rule" (4:26; cf. 4:31-32; 5:18-23, 25-28, 30).

The God who thus directs the fate of all nations is obviously superior to all other gods, and such epithets as "the great God" (2:45b), "the God of heaven" (ch. 2, *passim*), "the Most High" or "the Most High God" (3:26; 5:18, 21b; chs. 4, 7, *passim*), or even "the God of gods" (2:47; 11:36), seem entirely fitting. Frequently, His superiority to all other gods in power and occult revelation is more definitely stated (3:29; 4:3, 34-35; 5:23; 6:26-27).

Besides these ascriptions of universal and everlasting dominion, and of the power to do marvelous signs and to reveal secrets, we have a few touches of ethical characterization of this great God. "All His works are truth, and His ways justice," says Nebuchadnezzar (4:37; cf. 9:4, 7, 14, 16). The end in view in the calamity of the Jews is revealed as "to finish transgression, and to make an end of sins, and to make reconciliation for iniquity, and to bring in everlasting righteousness" (9:24). Yahweh may, however, be expected to show mercy (9:9a, 18b-19a).

This omnipotent and righteous God is the God of the Jews as a unique people. In contrast to "all the peoples, the nations, and the languages," the faithful Jews alone worship Him. Though the non-Jewish kings are caused to fear and honor Him, all the non-Jewish characters consistently regard Him as the God of Daniel and the other Jews, holding sway over all kingdoms but belonging only to this one people (e.g., 2:47; ch. 6, *passim*). Daniel, likewise, regards the all-powerful God as "my God" or "our God," the Jews as "thy people," and Jerusalem as "thy city" (6:22; ch. 9, *passim*).

Such a God can be counted upon to protect His own, the faithful among the Jews, and in a variety of ways He manifests His special guardianship over them. He causes Daniel "to find kindness and compassion in the sight of the prince of the eunuchs" (1:9). When Daniel and his companions pray for a revelation of Nebuchadnezzar's dream, in order not to perish with the rest of the wise men of Babylon, the God of heaven reveals the secret (2:18-19). Threatened with the fiery furnace, the three young Jews affirm their belief that their God is able to deliver them (3:17-18), and their loyalty to Him is fittingly rewarded when the fire leaves them wholly uninjured (3:27-28). Similarly, when the anxious King Darius calls into the lion's den: "O Daniel, servant of the living God, is thy God, whom thou servest continually, able to deliver thee from the lions?" (6:20), the faithful Jew can answer: "My God hath sent his angel, and hath shut the lions' mouths, and they have not hurt me" (6:22a).

The same protective power will eventually be experienced by those who are faithful to Yahweh in the writer's own day, though temporary suffering must precede the final deliverance (11:32-35; 12:1).

Not only deliverance, but dominion, is what God has in store for His faithful ones. They shall no longer be ruled; they shall rule all others. At the appearance of "one like unto a son of man" before the throne of the "ancient of days," "there was given him dominion, and glory, and a kingdom, that all the peoples, nations, and languages should serve him: his dominion is an everlasting dominion, which shall not pass away, and his kingdom that which shall not be destroyed" (7:13-14). This "one like unto a son of man" is apparently the representative of "the saints of the Most High." They "shall receive the kingdom, and possess the kingdom for ever, even for ever and ever" (7:18). Any attempt to destroy the saints of the Most High must eventually prove fruitless, since God has ordained their victory and rule (7:21-22, 25-27). Just as effectively as Daniel's enemies were destroyed (6:24), their great foe, Antiochus, will be overthrown. "They shall take away his dominion, to consume and to destroy it unto the end" (7:26).

The Yahweh of the book of Daniel is thus the righteous God of heaven, controlling the universe, the lives of all men and the fate of all nations. Though a recognition of His absolute supremacy is forced upon others, He is worshipped by only one people, He is the God only of the Jews. The faithful among His people this God will rescue from all misfortune, and exalt to everlasting dominion through the complete discomfiture of their enemies in some catastrophic dénouement of the drama of history.

Other Prophecies from the Second Century

DEUTERO-ZECHARIAH [1]

Perhaps the victories of the Maccabees furnish the background for the nationalistic prophecies now contained in Zechariah 9-11 and 13: 7-9.[2]

With Yahweh of hosts, the almighty warrior, fighting with them, His people will trample on their enemies. "For I have bent Judah for me, I have filled the bow with Ephraim" (9: 13a; cf. vss. 13b-16). "And they shall be as mighty men, treading down their enemies in the mire of the streets in the battle; and they shall fight, because Jehovah is with them" (10:5).

Yahweh will redeem His scattered people from all the countries (10: 6-12), and by His power they will have dominion over the neighboring nations (9: 1-7).[3]

In the midst of these oracles dealing with battle and the subjugation of enemies, comes the picture of the lowly, peace-bringing king, familiar through its use in the gospels. "He is just, and having salvation; lowly, and riding upon an ass," instead of upon a war-horse. "And I will cut off the chariot from Ephraim, and the horse from Jerusalem; and the battle bow shall be cut off; and he shall speak peace unto the nations: and his dominion shall be from sea to sea, and from the River to the ends of the earth" (9: 9-10).

The hope, then, is for a day when war among the nations will be unnecessary; but the way to its achievement, according to this prophet, is not a free relationship between equally honored nations, as in Isaiah 19: 18-25, but rather the universal dominion

---

[1] Only the first section of the book of Zechariah, like Isaiah, comes from the prophet whose name it bears. The latter chapters are from two anonymous writers who are often called, for convenience, "Deutero-Zechariah" and "Trito-Zechariah."

[2] Cf. Bewer, *The Literature of the Old Testament*, p. 420.

[3] A different note is struck when the prophet pronounces Yahweh's doom upon a certain unfaithful high priest. Yahweh will have to "awake" His sword against him; two-thirds of the people will have to perish, but the remaining third, refined by fire, will become a loyal people for Yahweh (11: 15-17; 13: 7-9).

of a just Jewish king. In the present, until that dominion is attained, Yahweh and His people must fight, and fight hard.

ISAIAH 33

In a time of great distress for the righteous (33:7-9), perhaps 162-1 B.C.,[4] Yahweh will arise and manifest Himself as a "devouring fire," "everlasting burnings," which terrify and consume the sinners, but leave the righteous unscathed (33: 13-16).

Then, in the happy future day, they "shall see the king in his beauty" (vs. 17); foreign domination will be thrown off (vss. 18-19); and in the free and quiet city of Zion Yahweh will dwell as Judge, Lawgiver, and King, over a people physically and morally sound (vss. 20-24).

TRITO-ZECHARIAH

Probably from about 135 B.C.,[5] come the prophecies that form the third section of the book of Zechariah (chs. 12-14, except 13:7-9).

Jerusalem, besieged by foes, will be made by Yahweh "a cup of reeling unto all the peoples round about" (12:2), and He "will seek to destroy all the nations that come against Jerusalem" (12:9). Elsewhere, it is anticipated that the besieging nations will be temporarily victorious, but "then Jehovah shall go forth, and fight against those nations, as when he fought in the day of battle" (14:3). Yahweh "will smite all the peoples that have warred against Jerusalem" with a horrible plague (14:12, 15), and after their defeat their wealth will be gathered in by Jerusalem (14:14).

The people left in these smitten nations could scarcely fail to recognize Yahweh's power. "Jehovah shall be King over all the earth" (14:9). In fact, they will come up to Jerusalem every year to worship Him at the feast of tabernacles (14:16) —to do Him homage, though hardly, it seems, to give Him a glad, voluntary allegiance, since they are forced to come "to worship the King" to save their country from drought or plague that would be sent by Him in punishment for failure to do so.

[4] Cf. Bewer, op. cit., p. 422.
[5] Cf. Bewer, op. cit., p. 424.

A God who uses His might, first to defeat the enemy nations, and then to compel all men to participate in His worship, is here depicted. Even a universal religion is not a very meaningful outlook, if its basis is divine force rather than divine love.

CHAPTER X

EDUCATIONAL IMPLICATIONS

1. Old Testament Resources for Education with regard to Peace and War—2. Suggestions as to Curriculum Policies

OLD TESTAMENT RESOURCES FOR EDUCATION WITH REGARD TO PEACE AND WAR

Is the God of the Old Testament a God of war? Yahweh nowhere appears as a God concerned only with war, like Mars, whose significance for mankind would be lost if organized fighting could be abolished. Even in the early poems, or the earliest hero tales in Judges, or such prophetic books as Nahum and Obadiah, in all of which Yahweh figures chiefly in warfare, it would be unfair to say that in the mind of the writer this was the only important attribute or function of his God. The essential character of the Hebrews' God abides through times when His people are at peace, and would stand if peace were indefinitely continued.

In the sense, however, of a God who Himself participates in battle, who instigates His own people or others to fight, who strengthens the side He approves, or in some way decrees the victor, and so can and does use warfare as an effective means of achieving His purposes, Yahweh has been found to be a God of war throughout most of the Old Testament material. In fact, the book of Ruth is practically the only entire document in which Yahweh is not directly or indirectly associated with warfare.[1] Occasionally, as in Jonah, it is only suggested by a vague threat of destruction, and the wisdom literature has only a few scattered references to it, but in the great majority of the Old Testament writings there is no uncertainty as to Yahweh's

---

[1] The Song of Songs, of course, is a secular anthology, and does not deal at all with Yahweh's relation to life. Esther does not mention Him, but our deductions as to His part in the story would not require our considering this an exception to the proposition regarding Yahweh's relation to warfare.

use of war. The distinction is that war is not here a good in itself, or per se a necessity for divine self-expression—but as the result of Yahweh's partisan interest in one people or as the result of His zeal for righteousness He is involved in struggle against those who oppose His purposes, and the generally accepted method in such a situation was to resort to warfare. Or, viewed from a slightly different angle, that Yahweh fights is the natural deduction from the fact of warfare in the experience of His chosen people, as long as the "progressive revaluation of values" has not wrought out and conceived as "respected and provided for" by God some social value inconsistent with warfare. Given the acceptance of the idea of Yahweh's participation in war, it is natural, further, that in the danger and excitement of battle His presence should be felt with peculiar vividness.

For educators to use these writings without historical background and independent ethical judgment, and hence to teach children that God instigates or uses warfare is, to say the least, not likely to develop aversion to war.

However, as indicated in the introduction, the problem involves much more than the mere question whether God makes use of warfare. We have tried to determine also whether the conception of God in any writing is such that belief in Him on the part of any social group would tend to induce attitudes that would engender war. The three tests proposed were the degree of impartiality in God's treatment of different nations, the nature of His attitudes toward men, and the methods used by Him in His dealings with men. We may now examine our findings on each of these three points.

In all the writings up to the time of Amos, and in some of the psalms, which may come from this earlier period, we seem to have plain henotheism. Yahweh is the God of the Hebrews alone, and, except insofar as His control over forces of nature gives Him wider influence, He does not dominate other peoples. Indeed, as late as the time of the Elisha stories, Yahweh seems to be a God associated with a definitely limited territory, as well as one of purely national interest. Other nations have their own gods, who are real entities possessing some power, though again and again shown to be inferior in power to the God of the Hebrews. The implications of such a henotheistic idea have been indicated in the introduction. The Yahweh of the Hebrews is, in relation to other nations, not essentially different from the Chemosh of the Moabites as represented by King Mesha in the inscription on the Moabite Stone. Impartiality in treatment of nations is not yet even a problem, for Yahweh has no dealings with other nations, except as He overpowers their gods and so enables His people to subjugate the others.

With Amos, we reach a new stage in the conception of Yahweh. As we have seen, through belief in a God of righteousness solely, he moves out beyond the limits of Israel and finds Yahweh dealing directly with other nations. The long line of prophets, historians, poets, and sages that followed Amos never relinquished the thought of a God in control of other peoples besides His own. The question as to how He treats other nations now assumes ethical significance.

The most common view in the Old Testament is that this God cares for only one nation, and that His dealings with others are therefore determined by what He purposes at the time concerning Israel. When His people please Him, any nation that blocks their progress is defeated and either destroyed or kept in subjection. If, on the contrary, they have been disobedient, other nations may be used as instruments of punishment. These nations may be required to recognize Yahweh's supremacy, an idea found frequently from Ezekiel on, and reaching a climax in Daniel, but they are of no worth in themselves and may be used or cast off as Israel's situation requires.

Against the background of this usual view, certain writings stand out as offering a different idea of Yahweh's relation to other nations.

The most challenging thought on this point is developed in Amos, Deutero-Isaiah, Jonah, and Isaiah 19:18-25. We have found that according to Amos Yahweh is practically impartial, and is about to punish all nations for unrighteous conduct.

Deutero-Isaiah uses the idea of Yahweh's special relationship with Israel, instead of declaring it annulled. Not impartial punishment for unrighteousness, but universal salvation to righteousness, is his theme, and Israel is to mediate the true moral religion to all nations. In Jonah, we have a concrete example of Yahweh's saving compassion for an enemy nation, which would justify the inference of a large degree of impartiality, and in the fragment in Isaiah 19:18-25 we reach the high point in the development of the idea of impartiality.

Besides these four outstanding contributions, a number of other writings portray Yahweh as desiring the worship of all peoples, though these vary greatly as to the nature of his concern for them. Some indicate that one day other peoples will be gathered in with the group of His own favored ones, as in a few passages in Zechariah, or in Isaiah 56:6-8, where the Temple is to become "a house of prayer for all peoples." In the interpolation in Zephaniah 3:9-10, Yahweh will give the peoples a "pure language" to worship Him. About six entire psalms, and several glosses in other psalms, represent Yahweh as worshipped and praised by all peoples, sometimes connoting universal gratitude for impartial beneficent acts, but elsewhere just homage in recognition of His marvelous works for the Jews. Trito-Zechariah's picture of the defeated nations compelled by Yahweh to participate in the Feast of Tabernacles at Jerusalem is almost void of significance here.

The wisdom literature gives a general impression of divine impartiality, through dealing with universal problems of individual life. In Job, the fact that the characters are non-Israelites strengthens this impression.

Besides portrayals of Yahweh's treatment of other peoples, we should note the human generosity toward foreigners found in varying degree in the Elisha stories, the J strand in Genesis, and the stories of Ruth and Jonah. Occasionally, too, we have marked a freedom from vindictiveness toward other nations where the situation might lead us to expect it, as in Isaiah 63:7-64:12 (almost entirely), Isaiah 21:1-15, and Isaiah 15-16.

In brief, Yahweh's interest and care seem equally limited in the early henotheistic stage and in the latest writings, with their absolute, transcendent, partisan deity. The writers who portray a wholly or partly universalistic conception come at various points between, and seem to represent individual protest against contemporary thought, rather than to indicate a steady development. These generous spirits may have influenced one another; they seem to have influenced the general trend of thought but little.

The degree of impartiality represented in Yahweh's treatment of different nations has an important bearing on the educational problem of developing warlike or peace-making attitudes. If the passages presenting a God who does not treat all nations alike are taught as giving a true conception of God for to-day, the pupils' natural inference is that they, too, need not regard all nations as equally important. In that case, their own would easily seem the most important. On the occasion of any clash of interests between nations, their own would be insisted upon, even at the expense of others. By that illogical transference repeatedly demonstrated, they come to think of God as entertaining for their nation the same partisan interest that He once had for the Hebrews. If the clash of interests leads to actual war, they may easily believe that God and their nation are fighting together, without dependence upon the ethical merits of the case.

If, on the other hand, passages presenting Yahweh's impartial dealings with all nations are stressed, and other ideas are frankly contrasted with this, with illustrations of their actual application, students may come to assume an attitude of equal regard for the rights of all nations, and to view their own as one among many nations all equally important in the divine plan, having no special claim upon God for assistance in enterprises that disregard the interests of others.

Turning now from the degree of impartiality to the nature of God's attitudes toward men, we should distinguish three somewhat related factors which enter into this conception—what He is considered to have done up to the present, what His purposes for the future are conceived to be, and what requirements He is thought to impose upon men.

In Old Testament thought, Yahweh is characteristically regarded as the sole cause, and the immediate cause, behind all events. Though men are usually represented as having power of choice,[2] the reins are never long out of Yahweh's hands, and in the last analysis good or ill fortune comes directly from Him.

The items of past experience most emphasized in the Old Testament are the liberation of the Hebrews from bondage in Egypt, their conquest of Canaan, success in war on various other occasions, and national greatness under David and Solomon. When such phases of history are stressed, the natural deduction is—a God who has sufficient power to achieve His purposes has been favorably disposed toward Israel. Yahweh's lovingkindness, His mercy, His gracious choice of this insignificant people to supplant others and attain unique blessedness, are all inferred from this past experience.

In spite of the tendency to emphasize this triumphant side, there were other sorts of past and present experience from which the Biblical writers deduced attitudes of Yahweh. Practically none of the generation that left Egypt actually reached the nearby land of Canaan, occasionally the Israelites suffered defeat in battle or even subjugation by another nation, and the climax of their national life was a two-fold experience of brutal capture and ignominious deportation. Was this their God's lovingkindness and tender mercy? Since God is conceived in anthropopathic terms, it is natural that in the parts of the historical writings dealing with these periods of misfortune, or in prophetic writings from times of impending calamity, such as Zephaniah, Jeremiah, part of Ezekiel, and Joel, or in writings coming out of the grief and horror of the actual experience of the capture of Jerusalem and the early exilic period, such as Lamentations, the Song of Moses, and many of the psalms, such attitudes should be ascribed to Him as wrath, indignation, anger (apparently used interchangeably), and, if the suffering is prolonged, unwillingness to heed cries for mercy.

The same process of deducing Yahweh's anger from the fact of disaster is found in many writings dealing with His attitude toward other peoples. To Nahum, to the authors of Isaiah 13-14

---

[2] We have found, also, the idea that Yahweh directly controls the conduct or the mental states of men, as when He keeps Abimelech from harming Sarah, or "hardens Pharaoh's heart," or sends an evil spirit upon Saul, or puts a lying spirit into Ahab's prophets.

and Jeremiah 50-51, and to Obadiah, the approaching destruction of Nineveh, Babylon, and Edom respectively give evidence of Yahweh's wrath against those nations—while several of Jeremiah's oracles of doom against neighboring nations, and the prophecies of the downfall of Egypt and Sidon in Isaiah 19:1-15 and 23:1-14 show such deduction even more clearly, since they are not so colored by the writer's own indignation and vindictiveness. Toward other nations, Yahweh may even cherish an inveterate antipathy, not just temporary anger.[3]

When we reach the point where the individual has relationship to Yahweh, apart from the social group, we find a similar inference of divine attitudes from past and present experience. Some of the psalms ascribe love and mercy to Yahweh because of personal deliverance from enemies or restoration to health. Other psalms, and the book of Job, deduce Yahweh's anger and hostility from the experience of personal suffering.

In this aspect of the conception of God, then, we have not the projection of the social ideal, but merely a logical deduction from experience viewed in the light of certain long-unquestioned dogmas.

In the other two factors suggested as entering into the formation of the conception of God's attitudes, we find, rather, the protest of a social ideal against past or present experience. Referring again to Professor Coe's discussion of the genesis of the idea of God, we have the proposition, already quoted in the introduction, that it is "a spontaneous, underived conviction that what is most important for us is *really* important, that is, respected and provided for by the reality upon which we depend." Now, it often happens that the values that have been wrought out of social experience seem not to be protected by the Power who is, by hypothesis, in immediate control of events. Faced with such a problem, the reasoning usually runs: God's ways are at times inscrutable; in the present He is either working out some subsidiary purpose or else biding His time; in either case, He will eventually act in vindication of those great values which, being most important to us, we must believe are most

[3] Cf., for example, Malachi's idea of His attitude toward Edom.

important to Him. The conception of God's ultimate purposes, then, enters in to prevent the necessity of interpreting Him solely on the basis of what He is thought to have done, or to have failed to do, in the past or the present.[4]

Faith in Yahweh's ultimate benevolence toward His chosen people usually leads, as in parts of Lamentations and Psalms, or in Isaiah 63: 7-64: 12, or in an apocalyptic writing like Daniel, to the ability to face terrible present distress with a great assurance of God's purpose soon to manifest His lovingkindness. Where Yahweh's peculiar relation to Israel is not given central value, as is the case with Amos and Micah (probably, in his original work), we find no expectation that doom will be averted or mitigated; whereas Hosea, Isaiah, Jeremiah, Ezekiel, and Deutero-Isaiah all transcend the actual or imminent calamity through some conception of divine attitudes of benevolence, lovingkindness, compassion, and forgiveness not at the time fully expressed in Yahweh's relations to His people, but based upon inference from certain of their past experiences and upon "the conviction that what is most important for us is respected and provided for by the reality upon which we depend." Each of the prophets mentioned arrived at his conviction in a unique way, and expressed it in his own terms, but the general idea of Yahweh's gracious future purpose which they had in common became a constant element in Hebrew thought.

Present suffering is thus viewed as disciplinary, rather than merely punitive—as a means to redemption, rather than an end in itself.

Since with most Old Testament writers the divine love has not been extended to other nations, Yahweh's future purpose need present no amelioration of present calamity for them; on the contrary, it is at times of their dominion or prosperity that the

[4] To save God's character by relinquishing the idea of His omnipotence—that is, to conceive of a finite, striving God, consistently representing the highest values, but not capable of achieving their complete expression without full human coöperation—is a solution of the problem sometimes offered to-day, but not in accord with Old Testament thought. Though, to be sure, we have frequently found, as in the J document or Hosea or Jeremiah, the idea that Yahweh is baffled for the time being by men's unresponsiveness and disobedience, still He always has the "whip hand," and His purpose cannot long be frustrated; by destruction of those who impede His way, or by punishment supposed to result in repentance, or by Himself giving men a new heart to obey Him, He will work His will.

conception of a further divine manifestation is required to offset a straight deduction from present conditions.[5]

We face the question of redemptive purpose with regard to individuals in the work of Ezekiel, the unknown writer of a large portion of Isaiah 56-66 (not "Trito-Isaiah"), and still more in the wisdom literature and many of the psalms. We find practically without exception that "the wicked" are considered beyond redemption—devoted to destruction. Except in Jonah, we do not find clear evidence of Yahweh's regard for the worth of every individual human life.[6]

From another point of view, however, the idea of the destruction of the wicked is itself an example of the mental process that we have been considering. Sometimes, as in Habakkuk, Job, Ecclesiastes, and certain psalms, it is not merely God's special favor and compassion that seem to be contradicted by present experience, but His very justice. Ecclesiastes becomes cynical in the face of the external impartiality of life, but in such a case the thinker may have recourse from the inscrutable present to a future of faith when the values believed to be represented by Yahweh will be vindicated. As long as the only sure indication of divine approval is considered to be some form of material success or tangible personal reward, as long as the righteous and the wicked are placed in two separate compartments of thought, almost like different species, and as long as human life per se does not represent a fundamental value, the idea of Yahweh's manifestation of His moral government of the world quite logically takes the form of a faith that He will eventually give the righteous the reward that they "deserve," and bring suffering, even complete destruction, upon the wicked.

The third main factor in any conception of God's attitude is the idea of what He requires of men. This has two aspects, which might be called the conservative and the creative.

On the one hand, when all goes prosperously, God's require-

[5] In its context, the interpolation in Zephaniah 3:9-10 does seem to refer to a redeemed remnant of all the nations upon whom the disastrous day of Yahweh is to come.

[6] Psalm 145:8-16 seems to assert it, but "all the wicked will he destroy" follows soon (vs. 20). It is perhaps involved in some of the universalistic writings that speak in terms of nations. Isaiah 25:6-8 suggests it also, but the context does not permit much stress on this thought.

ments may be regarded as fairly adequately met by the status quo. Certain individuals may need to be brought up to the level of the community—hence, these requirements may need to be reiterated from time to time, but on the whole we have here the tendency of religion to "sum up and represent social organization," and generally accepted social purpose, in the conception of God. This conservative aspect of the idea of God's requirements usually includes a large element of ritual along with ethical requirements.

The creative aspect has already been touched upon in the introduction. In this we have the "social protest" of an individual or group that has come to recognize as good something not adequately expressed in society. God, for this individual or group, is now considered to represent this value, among others, and so He must be requiring of society that it alter its life to give it a place. At this point we meet the ethical prophet, challenging society to heed the divine requirements of which he is absolutely certain but of which the rest of men are ignorant or careless. Such a person is likely to disparage everything that the unrighteous society is now valuing, and hence, frequently, to make a clean sweep of the cult and insist on morality alone as Yahweh's requirement. However, a creative step in the idea of God's demands may be taken also by one whose "revaluation of values" leads to giving a central place to the value of some ritual act not satisfactorily performed by people at present. In other words, the one who calls upon the people in the name of God "to like what they do not like" may be presenting to them a more exacting divine requirement in either the ethical or the cultic phase of religion.

The great majority of Old Testament writers portray a God with both ritual and moral requirements.[7] The cultic element is most prominent in the early stages of development and in the thought of the post-exilic period, in which the trend started by Ezekiel and the Holiness Code is carried on to its climax in the Priest Code, and Chronicles, as well as in the prophets from Haggai to Joel. The chief pre-exilic prophets, on the contrary, Amos, Hosea, Isaiah, Micah, and Jeremiah, definitely reject the

[7] Without enumerating the various requirements, we may note the fact that the restraint of anger and the kindness toward enemies occasionally urged among members of the community would be of significance for our problem if they should come to be extended beyond the national boundaries.

idea that the cult is of any vital concern to Yahweh, and place their whole emphasis upon His requirement of righteousness; Deutero-Isaiah has very little to say as to the ritual aspect of religion, and the author of Jonah seems to regard right conduct as sufficient. As we have seen, the insistence on nothing but moral requirements makes an approach to the thought of equality of nations easier than does the demand for the proper observance of a cult that, by hypothesis, has been revealed to only one people. The combination of a universalistic idea with a cultic emphasis can be obtained, however, by the assumption that other nations will one day be initiated into this particular cult. This is apparently the thought in those passages where Yahweh is to dwell in Zion in the future, but is to be worshipped by all men.

What people fall into the class of "the wicked," condemned by Yahweh, would, of course, depend upon the conception of His requirements. Infringement of cultic rules frequently offers opportunity for particularly dramatic instantaneous death, but Yahweh's doom for moral sin may be thought of as no less inexorable in the long run.

Amid all the variety of thought as to Yahweh's demands, one constant requirement is single-minded loyal obedience to Him. Expressed in anthropomorphic terms, Yahweh is a "jealous" God. "Anger" also appears frequently as a deduction, not from experience of calamity, as previously discussed, but from the contrast between actual conditions and Yahweh's supposed requirements. The natural reasoning is that if His people are doing what He abominates, He must be angry. This is the sort of divine anger that leads to threats of doom.

In the conceptions of Yahweh's attitudes toward men arising out of the three factors—actual past and present experience, idea of His future purpose, and idea of His requirements—we have found no steady progress in any direction. As in the case of the degree of His impartiality, the most significant development seems to come at some intermediate stage of thought, after which the general trend is back toward earlier emphases but a few scattered individuals still show in their writings a protest against the conceptions dominant in their times.

The educational implications of this study of the nature of Yahweh's attitudes have been suggested in the introduction. A God who is supposed to become passionately angry with men who displease Him, and to visit punishment in wrath, will not usually be regarded as condemning similar attitudes in human relationships. The assumption that His is always "righteous indignation" scarcely qualifies the general proposition, since few individuals or groups have ever thought of themselves, at the time of their anger, as *un*righteously incensed. If Yahweh is thus full of wrath against some nation, it is easy to conceive that He would welcome as His punitive instrument another nation whose people share His fierce but righteous anger. The only necessary step then is to identify as the object of divine wrath a certain nation against which we think we have a grievance—a step which history has often proved not to be difficult—and we have righteous war. Thus, to teach as an adequate representation of the God of to-day any material which portrays divine anger would be conducive to attitudes favorable to war.

When this idea of God's wrath is combined, as we have seen it to be in most of the Old Testament writings, with His failure to attribute essential value to human life outside the limits of a certain group, either the nation or "the righteous," there seems to be no deterrent to zealous participation in war on the part of those who adopt His attitudes.

On the other hand, the representation of Yahweh as embodying attitudes of lovingkindness and mercy and forgiveness, and as working out a compassionate redemptive purpose for men, tends to throw weight on the conception of the intrinsic worth of men and nations, and to make less acceptable the thought of destroying them. Passages where such attitudes on God's part are extended to all peoples would seem likely to strengthen in pupils a kindly and generous feeling toward other nations. The more numerous passages where attitudes of tender divine regard are appealingly portrayed, but applied only to Israel, might also be of use if pupils were stimulated to face frankly the question whether such limitation is in accord with their ideal of divine and human love.

Further, out of contact with the personalities who have taken creative steps in the development of the conception of God's moral requirements there might conceivably come some stimulus for similar creative thinking on the problems of the present day.

This brings us to a consideration of God's methods of dealing with men, as presented in the Old Testament.

Whether combined with a henotheistic or a monotheistic conception, a consistent element in the portrayal of Yahweh is His personal control of the separate phenomena of physical nature. Though the sort of purpose for which He uses the forces of nature is in each case of supreme importance, the fact of this control is also highly significant, since Yahweh is thus provided with an effective power to wield for the discomfiture or the blessing of the human beings with whom He deals. A God who can manipulate natural phenomena on every occasion has the possibility of being a God who depends upon might for the vindication of His purposes.

As a matter of fact, we have found an almost constant use of earthquake, eclipse, storm, wind, temporary separation of a body of water, plagues and pests of many kinds as the means to achieve Yahweh's ends. Terror, and usually destruction, are brought upon the ones against whom His face is set at the time— His own disobedient people, or, more frequently, their enemies. Of course, all that this really proves is that Yahweh, possessed of such weapons, is stronger than the human beings who oppose Him. That He is also in the right is constantly assumed, but such an assumption must be supported, if at all, by other evidence than the mere fact of His power to crush.

The other chief instrument of Yahweh's might is "the sword." The henotheistic Yahweh could wield this against other nations by directing His people's plan of attack and by strengthening them for the fray. When displeased with them, He could withdraw His aid in battle, and so let the enemy have free play against them. From Amos on, throughout the Old Testament, the divine dictator of the fate of all nations may move one against the other in whatever way He wills, using the army of any one as "His sword" against any other one. Here, again, the assumption is that He uses this clash of nations to work out purposes that are ultimately righteous, but no proof of this is inherent in the process itself, which shows only that one possessed of a stronger force can demolish others who are physically weaker.

Looking, now, at other methods ascribed to Yahweh besides the use of destructive might, we find, first of all, the frequent idea that Yahweh has refrained from the angry punishment merited at certain times by His disobedient people—that He has bestowed undeserved blessings, and has depended upon gratitude rather than fear as the response which will effectually motivate obedience. This thought is prominent in Deuteronomy, though the other occurs also, and it appears in many of the prophets, such as Amos, Hosea, Jeremiah, and Ezekiel, but is in each of these cases definitely combined with the idea that the people have failed to respond as Yahweh had hoped, and so He must resort to one of the methods of force just discussed.

Most prominent of the non-forceful methods is the conception of Yahweh's revelation of His will to chosen individuals, who are commissioned to try to awaken their fellows to a realization of His requirements and purposes for men. He gives His people every possible chance, "rising up early and sending" these prophets to point out the good and denounce the evil. It may be that they will heed, and turn from their wickedness before it is too late. In the utterances of the prophets, there is, of course, a large element of threatening, instilling fear of the imminent use of force by Yahweh. There is also, however, either explicit or implicit in most of the prophetic messages, a pleading and yearning, a challenging invitation, "Come, let us reason together." The writers of a code of laws may be animated by this same spirit. In that aspect of the prophet's function which represents God's efforts to make people "revalue values," recognize the good and understand why it is good, and so desire it and strive to attain it, we have a means of dealing with men which is ethically in an entirely different category from the compulsion of overwhelming physical power.

A step beyond the idea of mediating a divine message through the spoken or written word of a specially commissioned individual or group is the thought of a human life in all its relationships expressing the divine character. Though we find this conception much more definitely in the New Testament, we have beginnings of it in the Old Testament. The partial-incarnation method, as we have called it in the introduction, is used most clearly in Hosea's life. Just as his tragic experience with his wife is like Yahweh's heart-breaking experience with Israel, so his perseverance in love, his compassionate discipline and eventual redemption of his wife to faithfulness, are to be a revelation of the unquenchable love of Yahweh, ultimately capable of drawing Israel back to Him. Jeremiah represents the incarnation method much less. His refraining from the ordinary activities of life is to express a warning of coming calamity, rather than to demonstrate God's character. Though, looking back on his life, some people of a later day have seen in Jeremiah a divine attitude in his self-sacrificing persistence in what purposed to be a saving mission to his people, his imprecations on his enemies hardly look as though he thought of his suffering as revealing a sacrificial divine love. As a matter of fact, Jeremiah comes nearest to incarnation when he cries, "I am full of the wrath of Yahweh." Further examples of a partial incarnation conception are found in the thought of the ideal king, particularly as his character is depicted in Isaiah 9: 6-7; 11: 1-5; and 32: 1-2; in Micah 5: 1-4; in Jeremiah 23: 5-6; in Zechariah 9: 9-10; and in Psalms 2, 72, and 110. It is noteworthy that, on the whole, righteousness is the outstanding characteristic of this king—he will bring about justice in all the relations of men, and peace is frequently thought of as the crowning aspect of his régime. On the other hand, this representative of Yahweh is characterized by power, as well as righteousness. The extent of his dominion is a favorite theme, and, particularly in Psalms, we see that the divine endowment includes might to overwhelm those who oppose him.

Frequently Yahweh is thought of as about to rule directly over men, instead of through a royal representative. The fact of His reign does not in itself signify anything as to the methods used. He may on occasion exercise His rule through sheer force, but the idea is usually a deeper one. He, Himself, by an act of divine grace, changes the unresponsive hearts of His people so that they become gladly conformable to His will, as in Jeremiah or Ezekiel. Under this category comes the unique idea in Isaiah 2: 2-4, duplicated in Micah 4: 1-3, that His "ways," as exhibited in the life of His own people, will be so obviously superior to anything else known among men that all other nations will come of their own accord to learn of Him. Yahweh's method of achieving His will for mankind will then be a sort of arbitration among nations that voluntarily seek His judgments.

The divine method in the "servant poems" of Deutero-Isaiah remains to be considered. The association of these passages with the life of Jesus, and the idea of incarnation of the divine character in Jesus have been so essential a part of Christian thought through the centuries that it is quite easy to slip into the impression that Deutero-Isaiah regarded the "suffering servant" as incarnating the divine attitude. This, however, does not seem to be the case. Patient, non-resistant suffering, or, in fact, any keen suffering seems not to be a factor in the writer's conception of Yahweh Himself. Nevertheless, this does not detract from the extreme significance and uniqueness of the method which Yahweh is here considered to be employing to reach all nations—not might, but the drawing power of the vicarious suffering of His chosen servant-nation.

In the conception of divine method, as with degree of impartiality and nature of divine attitudes, there has been found no consistent trend of change throughout the material. The use of might is the most common method attributed to Yahweh from the earliest to the latest Old Testament writings, pleading through prophets is the next most frequent, and here and there occur other significant ideas.

As for the bearing of these ideas on education for or against war, it seems obvious that when Yahweh is regarded as relying upon might alone as the means of coercing a human group that opposes Him, whether that might is exercised through armies or through physical phenomena, He is acting upon the principle that underlies resort to arms on the part of an organized social group. When might settles a dispute, the will of the physically stronger is the "right" which becomes effective. If passages where Yahweh wins in conflict with men, without any satisfactory demonstration that His purpose is ethically superior to that of the opposing human beings, are used, without criticism, as educational material, what is to prevent the pupils' deduction that, with God, might makes right? If might makes right in God's relations with men, why should it not do so in men's relations with one another? Why should not the strongest nation enforce its will without compunction?

In practical effect, the case is not entirely different where the justice of Yahweh's position is indicated in the presentation, but His only method of achieving His righteous purpose is the use of physical force. No social group has ever found it very difficult to justify to itself its own prejudices and antipathies and ambitions, as well as its more or less frequent sense of injury. Any group emulating the methods of a God who depends solely on might to vindicate right would become involved in warfare almost as often as one holding that "might makes right."

Though no method, of course, carries within itself an assurance that the purposes for which it is used are ethically admirable, it seems as though the Biblical material in which God is represented as trying to persuade men, to make them desire what He desires and voluntarily devote themselves to His purposes, and the passages in which He reveals His righteousness or love through a human life, are rich in suggestion of possible human relationships that would substitute conference for battle and good-will for hatred. Moreover, if Deutero-Isaiah's ideal of non-resistant vicarious suffering as a means to international influence should be fully accepted by any group, that group could no longer consistently resort to warfare.

Finally, when Old Testament thought does value a condition of peace in the present order or glimpse a future day when the warfare of present experience shall be entirely abolished, what are the ideas as to the way to attain peace?

The most common idea is that dominion over all the neighboring nations is the only assurance of peace. David's conquests are the basis of the peace during Solomon's reign, and, in most of the portraits of Yahweh's specially anointed king, wide dominion, often universal dominion, is the prerequisite of peace. Even the lowly, peace-bringing king of Zechariah 9: 9-10 is to have dominion "from sea to sea," and everlasting dominion is the main gift to the "one like unto a son of man" in Daniel.[8]

[8] The hope of dominion has of course been found to be prominent in a great many other Old Testament writings, but peace as an ultimate good is not always explicitly associated with it.

Occasionally, as in Psalm 46, we find the kindred thought that Yahweh, by making His mighty works known among all nations, will cause wars to cease. We seem here still to have the idea of a peace maintained by force.

Isaiah believes that war in opposition to Yahweh's purpose is useless, and war in accordance with it is, for His people at least, needless, since His spiritual power is adequate to effect His ends. Yet, in the present, since there are wars, Yahweh uses them as a means of working His will.

In the Isaiah-Micah passage previously discussed, it is Yahweh's righteous and satisfactory arbitration among the nations in the future that will enable them to "beat their swords into plowshares." In Isaiah 11:6-9, the universal knowledge of Yahweh will result in the taming of all fierce and brutal tendencies, even among animals.

Though peace is not explicitly mentioned as the outcome of the mission of the suffering servant of Deutero-Isaiah, it would seem a reasonable corollary of the universal "justice" and "salvation" that he contemplates. This is actually realized in the remarkable passage, Isaiah 19:18-25, where international equality and friendship, and fellowship in worship, are the conditions of the coming day.

In much of this material, then, the basis of peace is a recognized inequality of national rights. Such a peace, resting upon dominion over other nations, would naturally have warfare and conquest as its prerequisites. If this ideal is involved in our educational material, it will need to be frankly analyzed and seen not to lead to peace in present-day practical application. A spiritual interpretation of these ideas of dominion is confusing unless the original sense is also recognized. The Old Testament passages, on the other hand, which represent free nations as voluntarily submitting their disputes to arbitration, thus making warfare unnecessary, or as enjoying intercourse based on mutual good-will and understanding, would seem to offer educational material likely to be provocative of peace-making effort.

We seem now to have found that certain parts of the Old Testament material do present a conception of Yahweh involving attitudes that would tend to engender war if ascribed to God by a social group to-day, and other parts portray a God, acceptance of whom would tend to stimulate ideas and attitudes conducive to peace. The bearing of biblical material upon the problem of attitudes toward war has seldom been a major consideration in the selection of passages for religious education, and most curricula in present use include both sorts of material, treated, frequently, without recognition of its implications in this regard. The time has passed when any religious educator can safely neglect to consider the relation of his work to this pressing problem. This study of the Old Testament writings has been undertaken with the hope that it may enable curriculum-makers to discover more readily what portions of the material are suitable for their purposes in respect to attitudes toward war, and to treat any part of the material in a manner likely to quicken the ethical discrimination of their pupils.

Suggestions as to Curriculum Policies

Out of the foregoing study, there emerge certain suggestions as to the selection and treatment of Old Testament material by those who desire to use it in a way that will influence attitudes with regard to war.

For curriculum-makers who aim to develop peace-making attitudes and aversion to war, the following policies might be suggested.

For younger children, all passages should be avoided in which God is represented as caring more for one group than for another, or as being angry and jealous, or as using His superior might to slay men.

For all grades, stress should be laid on the material which portrays God's interest in all peoples, His beneficence toward them, and His desire to have them know and love and serve Him—in brief, passages which present some aspect of divine impartiality. One should emphasize, also, material which shows God's redemptive rather than His punitive purpose—passages, therefore, in which divine love and forgiveness are prominent. Where possible, passages should be introduced that involve some other method of dealing with men than the destructive use of physical force.

For the more mature pupils, material should be used that presents different stages in the conception of God, but this should be treated in such a way as to stimulate ethical discrimination. Each part should be given its setting in the historical situation out of which it grew. The naturalness of change in religious conceptions, with changing experience, should be taught and frequently illustrated, but one should distinguish between mere change and progress. Where possible, provocative questions should be offered, instead of categorical ethical judgments, thus giving the pupils training in making their own moral discriminations.

Biblical material presenting generous and brotherly relations between men of different nations, and definite efforts to avoid war, should be utilized as well as passages explicitly portraying divine attitudes.

In general, the term "God" should not be used without qualification for any conception involving attributes not socially valid according to the highest ideals of the group whose educational aims the curriculum-maker is supposed to express. "The idea of God at that time" or "Yahweh as thought of by . . ." or some other discriminating phrase should indicate to the pupil that the conception under discussion may have been outgrown. Scrupulous care on this point would help to avoid the confusion in the pupils' minds now resulting from the tendency to characterize "God" in contradictory ethical terms in a series of lessons including material from different strata of thought.

One viewpoint with regard to ethical and religious values should be consistently expressed in a series of lessons if they are to be effective. If a character is lauded for kindness to enemies in one lesson, and in the same series men become heroes by virtue of wholesale slaughter, the point of either must be largely negatived by the other.

Material should be used from the most significant of the ethical prophets—for instance, Amos, Hosea, Isaiah, Jeremiah, Deutero-Isaiah, and Jonah—to a greater extent than is now done in most curricula.

The principles of international relationship involved in the material might be made clear by encouraging pupils to relate some incidents from the point of view of the non-Israelites concerned, or to paraphrase a prophet's message in present-day terms. Where possible, one should point out situations where the reversal of rôles results in a different attitude on the part of the writers—for example, the bondage of Israelites to the Egyptians, as compared with the bondage of Canaanites to the Israelites.

No memory passages should be used that will not feed the attitudes considered desirable. For instance, the imprecatory psalms should be avoided, or any others that identify "the enemy" with "the wicked."

In general, pupils should be stimulated to discover the original meaning of all passages used. If terms are allegorized or spiritualized in present-day usage, discrimination should be encouraged between this sense and the original one, and where possible the motive for the allegorization found. An example would be the "spiritual enemies"—besetting sins, and so on—often read into psalms that referred originally to concrete human enemies.

On the other hand, curriculum-makers would seem to be developing attitudes conducive to war by selecting or treating their material with the following emphases.

It may be assumed that "we," as a limited group—whether a church or a nation or a race—have become a "chosen people," and have inherited the special divine favor shown to the Jews in any part of the Old Testament.

Biblical material may be treated as though it all represented the same stage of ethical development, and, as a corollary of this, all passages portraying the character of God may be treated as though they were supplementary, never contradictory. For example, no sharp distinction may be made between the God of Deutero-Isaiah or of Jonah and the God of Deborah or of Joshua or of Obadiah. He may be called just "God" in every case, thus making it easier for the pupil throughout his life to shift into whatever conception of God best suits the mood of the moment, without being definitely conscious of such changes.

Stories may be chosen for their dramatic quality and their appeal to the ideals of the brave and heroic already picked up by the children from their outside experience. The warrior type of hero may be particularly stressed, and courageous or momentous exploits in war may be depicted with special vividness, such as Samson's slaughter of the Philistines, David's fight with Goliath, and the wiping out of the Canaanite cities during the Conquest period.

Great religious value may be attached to striking exhibitions of divine might, with the assumption that the object for which it is used is always admirable. Material capable of such treatment is found, for instance, in the Egyptian plague stories, the drowning of the Egyptians at the Red Sea, the impressive revelation of Yahweh in lightning and earthquake at Sinai, the defeat of Sisera's army at the River Kishon, and the slaying of the South-Canaanite armies by Yahweh's great hailstones.

One may always adopt the point of view and the ethical judgments of the writer of a Biblical account, and not encourage pupils to regard an incident from the point of view of a person or group condemned in the story.

For memory passages, one may draw largely upon the psalms that express confidence in Yahweh's (or God's) protection from enemies. It may be suggested that we all have "enemies of some kind" to overcome. Occasionally, one may show with enthusiasm how these psalms have inspired armies in the past, and imply or state that those armies were fighting with God against the wicked. In such a case, one would not be likely to take illustrations from both sides of the same war, but would probably accept the usual judgment of the group as to which side was God's side.

Biblical passages that might stimulate pupils to question the rightness of war may be entirely omitted from the course.

In the opinion of the present writer, many of the curricula in current use in religious education are doing things suggested in this last section as likely to be conducive to attitudes favorable to war, though usually, probably always, such a purpose is far from the thought of the curriculum-makers.

BIBLIOGRAPHY

This list includes only books to which reference has been made.

BADÉ, WILLIAM FREDERIC. *The Old Testament in the Light of To-day.* Boston and New York, Houghton Mifflin, 1915.

BARTON, GEORGE A. *Archæology and the Bible.* Philadelphia, American Sunday-school Union, revised edition 1925.

BEWER, JULIUS A. *The Literature of the Old Testament in Its Historical Development.* New York, Columbia University Press, 1922.

BEWER, JULIUS A. *International Critical Commentary* on *Jonah.* New York, Scribners, 1912.

BEWER, JULIUS A. *International Critical Commentary* on *Obadiah* and *Joel.* New York, Scribners, 1911.

BRIGGS, CHARLES AUGUSTUS. *International Critical Commentary* on *The Book of Psalms*, 2 volumes. New York, Scribners, 1907.

BRIGHTMAN, EDGAR SHEFFIELD. *The Sources of the Hexateuch.* New York, Abingdon Press, 1918.

CADBURY, HENRY J. *National Ideals in the Old Testament.* New York, Scribners, 1920.

COE, GEORGE ALBERT. *The Psychology of Religion.* Chicago, University of Chicago Press, copyright 1916.

FOWLER, HENRY THATCHER. *A History of the Literature of Ancient Israel.* New York, Macmillan, 1912.

GILBERT, GEORGE HOLLEY. *The Bible and Universal Peace.* New York, Funk and Wagnalls, 1914.

HARPER, WILLIAM RAINEY. *International Critical Commentary* on *Amos* and *Hosea.* New York, Scribners, 1905.

KENT, CHARLES FOSTER. *Israel's Historical and Biographical Narratives,* Vol. II of *The Student's Old Testament.* New York, Scribners, 1905.

MCGIFFERT, ARTHUR CUSHMAN. *The God of the Early Christians.* New York, Scribners, 1924.

MITCHELL, HINCKLEY G. *International Critical Commentary* on *Haggai* and *Zechariah.* New York, Scribners, 1912.

MOORE, GEORGE FOOT. *The Book of Judges,* Part 7 of *The Sacred Books of the Old and New Testaments,* Polychrome Edition (ed. Paul Haupt). New York, Dodd, Mead, 1898.

POLLOCK, CHANNING. *The Enemy.* New York, Brentano's, 1925.

SMITH, HENRY PRESERVED. *International Critical Commentary* on *Samuel.* New York, Scribners, 1902.

SMITH, J. M. POWIS. *International Critical Commentary* on *Malachi.* New York, Scribners, 1912.

SMITH, J. M. POWIS. *International Critical Commentary* on *Micah, Zephaniah,* and *Nahum.* New York, Scribners, 1911.